Beyond Green
A Case Study House for the 21st Century

Other books by Peter Jon Pearce:

Structure in Nature is a Strategy for Design

Curved Space Diamond Structure

Polyhdera Primer

Experiments in Form

Beyond Green
A Case Study House for the 21st Century

The Architecture of the *Pearce Ecohouse*

Peter Jon Pearce

PEARCE PUBLICATIONS

Beyond Green
A Case Study House for the 21st Century

The Architecture of the *Pearce Ecohouse*

Peter Jon Pearce

For more information on the work of
Peter Jon Pearce visit:

www.pjpearcedesign.com

Book design: Peter Jon Pearce

Printed by CreateSpace, an Amazon.com company.

Available from Amazon.com and other retail outlets.

To my dearest Susie:

We will build this!

Acknowledgements

This project has been underway for some time now. My wife, Susan, and I purchased the property for the building site in the Santa Monica Mountains in 1990, and have been contemplating this project ever since. The concept of the *Pearce Ecohouse* began to take shape almost immediately after the purchase of the property, and the schematic design was nearly fully formed by the end of 1996. That was the 10% inspiration part, and since then it has been the 90% perspiration of the details of the design, site planning, and product development. As might be expected, other priorities intermittently took priority over this project, especially since this has been strictly a labor of love. Since 1996, other significant projects have been developed including my successful *Cachet* chair manufactured by Steelcase, Inc. For a complete survey of my work history, please visit my web site: pjpearcedesign.com.

Since the early 1990's, as friends and respected colleagues have become aware of this project, a number of people have been very interested and supportive of this radical approach to residential design. This has been very meaningful to me, particularly as the duration and scope of the project has expanded. I have been encouraged to press on by this support. For their interest, enthusiasm, and belief in this project I would like especially like to thank Ralph Knowles, Dale Fahnstrom, Carol Burke, Kathy and Baylis Glascock, Marilyn Neuhart, Mike Bank, Roger Conrad and Karen Reeser. For his wonderful visualizing computer renderings, I would also like to thank Jim Walters. I would also like to acknowledge, posthumously, Carlos Diniz, Sam Hurst, Niels Diffrient, and John Neuhart, who were each a source of encouragement and belief in the *Pearce Ecohouse* project.

I would also like to thank my brother Mallory and sister Penny, for their love and support through the very many years since we were all young.

As a special note, I would like to acknowledge the inspiration that I gleaned from the work of Charles Eames, Konrad Wachsmann, Buckminster Fuller, D'Arcy Wentworth Thompson, Joseph Paxton, R. J. Mitchell, Malcolm Sayer, and Erwin Komenda. The seminal work of each of these individuals reinforces a design ethos that validates my axiom: *form as an agent of performance.*

I would also like to thank Toby Cowan for his support and guidance in the realm of document design, preparation, and publication. Finally, I would like to thank my two daughters, Celia and Aleta, for their belief in me and this project. Above all, I want to thank my loving wife, Susie, for her enthusiasm, energy, and unwavering commitment to this radical design paradigm-shift that I call the *Pearce Ecohouse*. She is my "high-tech mama"!

Peter Jon Pearce
Malibu, California
July 2015

Part 1: Underpinnings

Introduction   3

Prototype Residence
Case Study House
Early Influences
Half the Energy
Early Warning
Moral Imperative
Green Design
Radical Alternative
Higher Standards
High-Performance
Paradigm Shift
Building is Backwards
Style and Profit
Irrational Sensibilities

Understanding First Principles   11

High Performance Design Applications   13

1981: Solar Canopy, Jeddah International Airport
1982: American Airlines Corporate Headquarters
1982: Playground for All Children
1983: California State Building, Shade Canopy
1985: British Columbia Pavilion, Expo '86
1985: Seventh Market Place, Shopping Mall
1986: Fallbrook Mall and Food Court
1992: Southland Gardens Mall, Winter Garden
1993: Universal CityWalk
1995: Navy Pier Reconstruction, Chicago
1995: Fremont Street Experience

Part 2: Design Strategy

Guiding First Principles   23

Design Strategy

Purposes of Shelters   24

Climate Management
Spatial Differentiation
A Sense of Well-Being

Physical Principles of Climate Management   **26**

Solar Radiation: Source of Heat Gain
Temperature Differential: Source of Air Movement

Attributes   **28**

Architecture   **29**

Environmentally Friendly Architecture
Design Simplicity
Solar Power
Minimum Site Intervention
Preservation of Native Plants
Serving Needs of Residents
Metaphorical Barn
Design Vocabulary
Form as an Agent of Performance
Strength of Geometry
Accommodating Climate Parameters

Beyond Prefab   **33**

Renewed Interest
Building Materials
Building Components

Structure, Materials, and Process   **34**

Material Attributes
Prefabricated Components
The 80/20 Phenomenon
Steel Strut Components
Exoskeleton
Space-truss Deck
Interior Floor System
Electrical and Network Distribution
Exterior Floor System
Glass Enclosure
Glass Panels
Virtually Airtight
Outboard Sprinkler System
Concrete Piers

Architecture as Product Design   **39**

Factory Made
Computer Aided Design

Climate Management Strategies   **40**

No Air Conditioning Required
Intercepting Solar Heat Gain
Capturing Solar Heat Gain
Orientation
Thermal Mass
Radiant Heating and Cooling
Geothermal Heat Exchanger
Summary of Cooling Principles
Insulated Glass
Minimal Surface
Natural Light

Site Development and Landscaping   **47**

Semi-Wilderness
Mediterranean Climate
Drought Tolerant Plants
Fire Ecology
Natural Habitat
Fire Hazards
High Density
Density Reduction
Abusive Development
Ecosystem Friendly

Part 3: Visualizing the *Pearce Ecohouse*

Visualizing the *Pearce Ecohouse*   **53**

The Project Site   **54**

Google Earth Montages   **53**

Photomontage   **55**

Adaptation to Site   **58**

Matching Contours of the Building Site   **61**

Walking Around the *Pearce Ecohouse*   **66**

Site Construction and Assembly   **74**

Completing Construction   78

Photovoltaic Solar Collectors
Radiant Heating and Cooling
Waste Management System
Interior Finishing
Driveway

The Glass Enclosure   80

Glazing Panels
Outboard Sprinkler System
Overhead Louvers

Climate Management Canopy   85

Interior Views of Solar Radiation Management   88

Monthly Performance: Images
Sun Angle Reciprocities

Project Plan, Elevations, Sections, Views   96

Plan
Elevations
Sections
Views

Residence Only Views   106

Plan
Elevations
Views
Sections

Garage Views   114

Views
Elevations
Plans
Sections

Access Deck View   120

Plan
Views

Revisiting the Design Elements   122

      Building Spaces
      Building Enclosure
      Upper Level
      Lower Level
      Detached Garage
      Photovoltaic Array
      Interior Floor Cladding
      Exterior Deck Cladding

Interior Visualized   126

      Upper Level Residential Space
      Lower Level General Purpose Space

Exploded Views   138

Achieving Closure   139

      Scope of Work
      Rational Alternatives
      Modest House
      Sense of Well Being
      Moral Obligation

Part 1

Underpinnings

Part 1
Underpinnings

Introduction

Prototype Residence

This document is a preview of a building development project called the **Pearce Ecohouse**. The goals of this project will be enumerated in what follows, along with a presentation of how these goals manifest themselves as physical design. The over arching concern of this project is to develop a prototype residence, which establishes the highest possible standards of sustainability for the design of buildings.

The client for this project is my wife Susan and myself. I am also the designer, architect, product designer, engineer, manufacturer of record, and building contractor. The content of this project is driven and controlled by our personal vision of what a house could be, setting aside all preconceived notions of residential design. It is an opportunity to demonstrate a solution unencumbered by agendas and constraints that conspire against the true potential of our vision.

Case Study House

We are calling this project a *Case Study House for the 21st Century* as an homage to the post World War II, mid-century, Case Study House Program. This program was created by John Entenza, publisher and editor of *Arts and Architecture Magazine*, which sponsored the Case Study House project of the mid-20th Century. Many innovative modernist homes were designed and built in the period from 1945 to 1966. There were 36 homes altogether. They were considered prototypes for a new approach to residential design in the post war period. The most influential Case Study House for me was the Eames House. I went to work for Charles Eames in 1958 upon graduation from the Institute of Design in Chicago. At that time, I was not familiar with the Case Study House program.

The Eames House, 1950. Designed by Charles and Ray Eames as part of the influential Case Study House program.

The Crystal Palace, London, 1850. Designed by Joseph Paxton. Can be considered the first systems building on a large scale, built entirely from a pre-fabricated cast iron kit-of-parts.

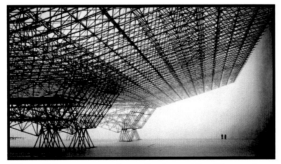

Aircraft hanger system designed by Konrad Wachsman c.1950, for the U.S. Airforce. The project was never built but demonstrated the potential of large space truss systems exhibiting high strength to weight assembled from standardized tubular steel components.

Indeed, I was unaware of the Eames House when I joined the Eames office. Though I was mostly involved in seating design I quickly became aware of the Eames house. Of course, on many occasions, I had the opportunity to visit this seminal house assembled from industrially produced standard steel components. The Eames house was clearly assembled from a kit-of-parts, which, for me, was one the most interesting things about its design. Of all of the Case Study Houses this remains the most interesting from a consideration of its construction method. More than any other of the mid-century Case Study Houses, the Eames house demonstrated the idea of building from a kit-of-parts. To that extent it certainly had a profound influence on my thinking.

The Eames House adapted standard steel industrial construction materials to its design form. Our *Pearce Ecohouse* takes the idea of a kit-of-parts to a new level of sophistication. The *Pearce Ecohouse* construction is based on purpose designed components specifically manufactured for the project. It is a true building system, for which the *Pearce Ecohouse* is a true prototype. Once the prototype is actually built and tested, the components from which it is assembled can be readily reproduced to be used in subsequent residential construction.

More generally, the mid-century Case Study houses profoundly demonstrated the idea of open plan design, with the generous use of glass to enhance interior living with natural light and access to nature. Such attributes were enabled by the forthright use of steel frame structures.

Certainly the attributes of kit-of-parts technology, open plan design, the generous use of glass, and steel construction have had a strong influence on the conception and design of the *Pearce Ecohouse*. In some ways our project could be considered an evolutionary step in a new modernist vision of residential design. The *Pearce Ecohouse* assimilates the lessons of Joseph Paxton's 1850 Crystal Palace, the Eames House, the ideas of Konrad Wachsmann, and the structural work of Buckminster Fuller.

4

The Buckminster Fuller designed 250 foot diameter geodesic at the 1967 world's fair at Monteal. Fuller demonstrated structural principles that are scale and material independent with a great number of domes.

The first prototype of the Spitfire flew in 1936. Designed by R.J. Mitchell, this was one of the greatest fighter planes of WW I I. New levels of performance were achieved by this aircraft.

The Porsche 356 first reached production in 1949, designed by Erwin Komenda, set new standards of aerodynamic and structural efficiency. The car would go 93 mph with only 40 hp, and achieved great fuel economy.

The D Type Jaguar endurance racer was designed by aerodynamicist Malcolm Sayer. This car won Le Mans three years in a row (55,56,57), taking advantage of its refined and unprecedented low drag form.

Early Influences

Other early influences from the non-architectural realm include the work of R.J. Mitchell, the designer of the British Spitfire airplane, c.1936; Erwin Komenda, designer of the Porsche 356, c.1949, and Malcolm Sawyer, the designer of the Jaguar C Type and D Type, both of which won the Le Mans 24 hour race in the 1950's. The C Type won in '51 and '53, and the D Type in '55, '56 and '57.

These purpose built objects exemplify a concept that I call *form as an agent of performance*. High performance design manifesting a complete integration of form, structure, materials, and process, in which the unprecedented performance of these vehicles is directly attributable to their form. These designs directly impacted my design sensibilities at a young age, before I had any interest in building design. Although these examples represent pinnacles of high performance design, there is no denying their enduring beauty.

The concept of *form as an agent of performance* and its corollary *high performance design* will be discussed later in this book. A deeper and more detailed presentation of these early influences will have to wait for a subsequent book. As we will show, high performance design is a key strategy for the achievement of sustainability in building design. To that extent these early influences have surprising relevance.

Half the Energy

Approximately half of the world's energy is consumed in the construction, operation, and maintenance of buildings. This means that buildings are major contributors to our dependence on fossil fuels, and, therefore, major contributors to environmental pollution and global warming. Further, we are rapidly approaching a crisis in which the global economy will not be sustainable in its present fossil fuel based, waste intensive model. Nothing short of a new world order will be required, based on an energy efficient ethic and the widespread adoption of non-depletable energy sources.

Early Warning

In the February 4, 1949, issue of *Science* magazine, M. King Hubbert presciently warned us that "It is upon our ability to … evolve a culture more nearly in conformity with the limitations imposed upon us by the basic properties of matter and energy that the future of our civilization largely depends." The Hubbert article addresses the transformation from a low-energy agrarian culture to a high-energy industrial culture.

Hubbert shows that the reliance on fossil fuels by our industrial culture will be, of necessity, a short-lived history since these are exhaustible resources. Unfortunately, the world ignored Hubbert, and, as a consequence, we now find ourselves in impending crisis. Our reliance on fossil fuels for energy is polluting the earth, and will eventually lead to energy shortages. The pollution has given rise to global warming, the implications of which are unthinkable, which is probably one reason why we are in such denial about this issue. The fuel shortages will give rise to serious global economic stress. Perhaps this is good thing, since it may inspire rational problem solving in the energy arena. It has been said, "that necessity is the mother of invention."

It is reasonable to conclude that global warming is the most serious problem, among a collection of other serious problems, impacting planet earth. At the very least rising seal levels will devastate communities world wide, with unimaginable consequences.

Moral Imperative

One concludes from these circumstances that the goal of sustainability in building design is a moral imperative. Of course, what may exemplify sustainability in design is subject to interpretation. Sustainability has become a trendy word in some design circles, but much of this attention seems to lack real depth, and is, perhaps, too cautious in its response.

Fly-around of the *Pearce Ecohouse,* showing different views of the residential structure. The computer model reveals the building geometry and supporting piers, without the site. The **Climate Management Canopy** is prominent in these images.

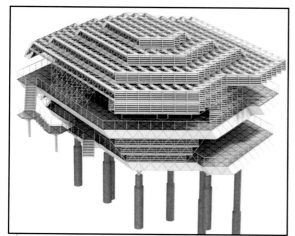

View from the northwest.

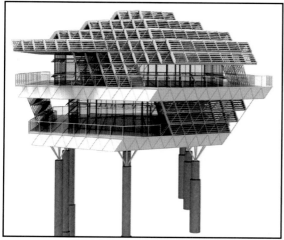

View from the east.

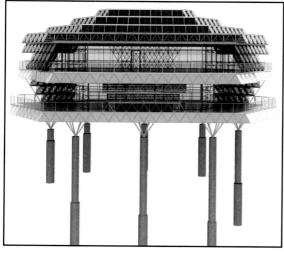

View from the north.

Green Design

Currently, in the architectural community and residential building, in particular, the term "green design" is often evoked to suggest an energy efficient solution that promises some level of sustainability. Although many of these projects have merit, most are constrained by conventional building methods and preconceived notions of what a house or building ought to look like. Because of such constraints, the effectiveness of such solutions tends to be very limited. Energy efficiency may be improved, but only incrementally.

Radical Alternatives

What is needed in building design, if there is any chance of truly creating a sustainable future, are radical solutions - a paradigm shift. We will need transcendent solutions that set aside sentimental, nostalgic, and self-conscious approaches to architecture. In the same way, we need radical solutions for all aspects of energy efficiency and pollution control. For example, higher fuel economy standards for automobiles need to be imposed immediately as we continue to explore and implement alternative energy sources.

Higher Standards

The goal of the *Pearce Ecohouse* project is to achieve higher standards of energy efficient sustainability over the typical "green design" approach. This becomes a "beyond green" mandate unconstrained by conventional building methods, materials, and design mannerisms. It means looking at building design - in this case residential design - without the baggage of house *style.* It means that, given what is technically possible, what could a house be, if designed from the inside out, from a perspective of high-performance? What could a house be if designed as a high-performance product based upon readily available materials and manufacturing processes? Green design tends to be too modest in its manifestations. We need a radical approach – a paradigm shift – that takes energy efficient building to a much higher level.

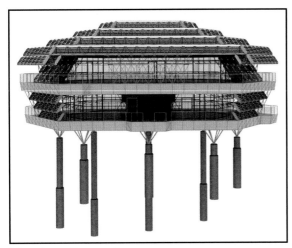

View from the south.

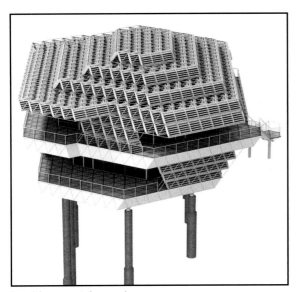

Looking east from above.

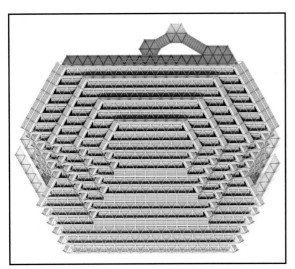

Plan view.

High-Performance

My strategy for achieving the goals summarized in the foregoing is what I call *high-performance design*. By that I mean design in which form, structure, process, and materials, are fully integrated to create products of exceptional performance, material efficiency, long life, and enduring appearance. It is a strategy, which considers **form as an agent of performance**, and is seen as a fundamental condition for the achievement of real sustainability in the built environment. I have been pursuing this strategy for 50 years.

In an attempt to demonstrate this high-performance design strategy, I have designed a technically advanced residence - the **Pearce Ecohouse**. Informed by everything I have learned in over 50 years of working as a designer, I have envisioned a residence that takes energy efficiency to a very high level - **beyond green**.

Paradigm Shift

This project represents a paradigm shift, unconstrained by legacy of craft based building methods, which dominate the world of building design, especially residential architecture.

Building is Backward

The building arts, particularly as manifested in residential building in the US, are anachronistic in the extreme. This is in contrast to virtually all other product creating enterprises of human culture. The building arts are dominated by concepts that contradict a high-performance design ethos. By contrast, a high-performance design ethos dominates the design of almost everything else, including aircraft (as necessity dictates), computers, consumer electronics, consumer appliances, and even automobiles. In such applications history has inexorably demonstrated higher performance at lower cost, except in the building arts including home furnishings.

8

Style and Profit

The lack of high performance innovative design approaches remains something of a mystery. This is no doubt attributable in part to cultural factors having to do with the striving for status. So many people seem to be extremely sentimental and unimaginative about their domicile design and home decoration. Most domestic architecture is not really designed, but created by developer/builders, without serious efforts to deal with climate management and energy efficiency. The residential building industry is all about style and profit, with a shocking lack of vision or any sense of social responsibility.

Irrational Sensibilities

Although there are many examples of high-performance energy efficient automobiles, it is a field dominated by odd and irrational sensibilities. It is a design environment dominated by style and fashion, and not fundamental design concepts. The automotive industry is so large and potentially profitable (for many companies), it is driven by marketing strategies rather than any socially responsible ethic. The popularity of SUV's is an example of a vehicle that has become an irrational fad and agent of status. It may have started as a specialized utility vehicle, e.g. Range Rover, but certainly makes little sense as daily urban transportation.

Residential building, especially in the US, is vulnerable to the same irrational sensibilities, where concerns for "style" and "mannerism" are the dominant drivers of building "design". The same criticism can be leveled at much of architecture, even commercial buildings and "high design", where serious efforts to embrace sustainability are surprisingly rare, with some notable exceptions.

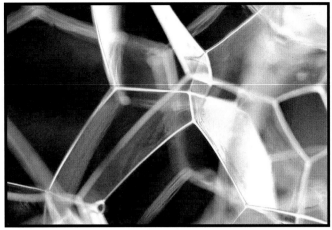
Soap Bubbles: Surface to volume is minimized.

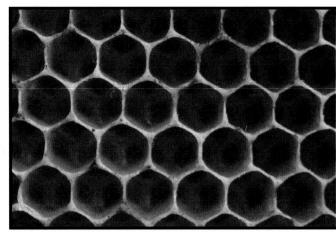
Honeycomb: Most honey with least bee's wax.

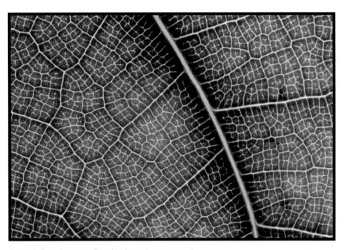
Leaf Surface: Optimized network.

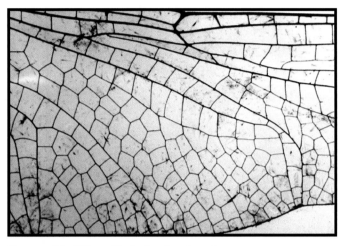
Dragon Fly Wing: Optimized network.

Snow Flakes: Least energy infinite variation.

Platinum: Dense and stable packing of atoms.

Natural structure exhibits patterns of least energy and optimized structure. In nature form is an energy conserving diagram of forces - **form is an agent of performance**. In nature arbitrariness of form is minimized through adaptation to the environment - through *natural selection*. Form giving in nature is the prototype for high-performance design, the embodiment of first principles. The *Pearce Ecohouse* draws both inspiration and specific technical ideas from the study of the least energy patterns found in nature.

10

Understanding First Principles

My high-performance design strategy has been driven by a restless quest to discover and understand *first principles*. In any given problem-solving effort, what are the underlying and immutable principles, independent of cultural bias, which truly govern optimum design possibilities? It is a strategy that continues to guide my design efforts today.

My book, *Structure in Nature is a Strategy for Design*, The MIT Press, 1978, 1990, is about this effort to discover and understand first principles, as they inform an understanding of the structure and morphology of possible building system design. This work formed the theoretical basis of my future work in the design, engineering, manufacture, and installation of over 80 state-of-the-art architectural projects, from approximately 1980 to 1995. These projects comprise a significant part of the application side of my learning experience - the practical experience in high-performance design.

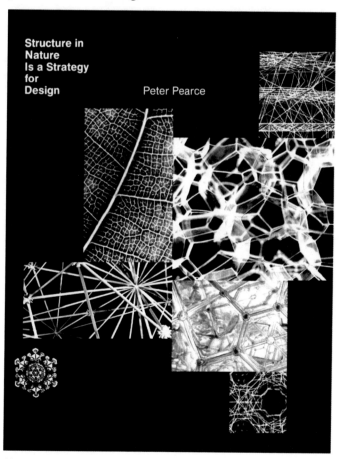

New copies of this book are available from the author's inventory through amazon.com

Five structures: overview

Agricultural Biome

Wilderness Biome: 180 foot clear span

Wilderness Biome: Interior

Habitat: Residence, Offices, Dining

Nine Intersecting Vaults During construction

Biosphere 2, Ecosystem Laboratory: 1985-1990

Five Structures: five acre footprint; seven million cubic feet of airtight volume; approximately 80,000 tubular steel struts, assembled into structures clad with a steel-framed glazing system, and sealed with silicone caulking. This project was designed, engineered, manufactured, and installed by Pearce Structures, Inc., a company dedicated to the implementation of high-performance structural and enclosure systems at architectural scale. The Company operated out the Los Angeles, California area from 1980 to 1995, when it closed its doors.

High Performance Design Applications

Around 1980, I formed a company called *Pearce Structures*, where, in collaboration with architectural firms, over 80 projects were designed and built comprising approximately 2 million square feet of surface area. These projects involved the application of optimized space-truss structures to a wide variety of building projects. Such projects often included integral glazing/cladding systems and climate management attributes. These projects were characterized by innovative geometries, structural solutions, and building components, all designed, engineered, and manufactured by *Pearce Structures*.

Many of these projects are shown on the following pages.

Perhaps the most well known of these projects was *Biosphere 2*, in Arizona, completed in 1990.

Other major projects from this period include:

1981: Solar Canopy, Jeddah International Airport, Saudi Arabia

1982: American Airlines Corporate Headquarters, Texas

1982: Playground for All Children, Flushing Meadows, New York

1983: California State Building, Shade Canopy, Van Nuys, CA

1985: British Columbia Pavilion, Expo '86, Vancouver, B.C.

1985: Seventh Market Place, Shopping Mall, Los Angeles, CA

1986: Fallbrook Mall and Food Court, Woodland Hills, CA

1992: Southland Gardens Mall, Winter Garden, Taylor, Michigan

1993: Universal CityWalk, Los Angeles

1995: Navy Pier Reconstruction, Chicago

1995: Fremont Street Experience, Las Vegas, Nevada

1981: Solar Canopy, Jeddah International Airport, Saudi Arabia, Architect: Richard Schoen, RSA

1982: American Airlines Corporate Headquarters, Texas, Architect: William Pereira Associates

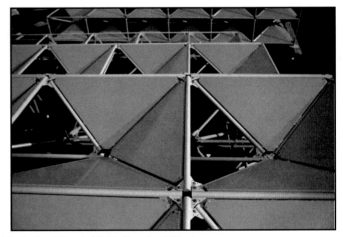

1982: Playground for All Children, Flushing Meadows, New York, Architect: NYC Dept. of Parks

1983: California State Building, Shade Canopy, Van Nuys, CA, Architects: PC Architects

1985: British Columbia Pavilion, Expo '86, Vancouver, B.C., Architect: Waisman, Dewar, Grout

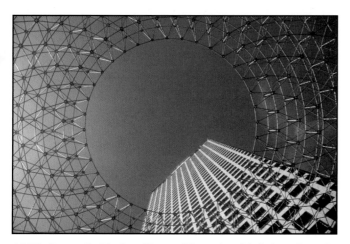

1985: Seventh Market Place, Shopping Mall, Los Angeles, CA, Architect: The Jerde Partnership

1986: Fallbrook Mall and Food Court, Woodland Hills, CA, Architect: Charles Kober Associates

1992: Southland Gardens Mall, Winter Garden, Taylor, Michigan, Architect: Morris Architects

1993: Universal City Walk, Los Angeles, Architect: The Jerde Partnership

1995: Navy Pier Reconstruction, Chicago, Architects: Ben Thompson Architects & VOA Architects

1995: Fremont Street Experience, Las Vegas, Architect: The Jerde Partnership

Part 2

Design Strategy

Part 2
Design Strategy

Guiding First Principles

Design Strategy

The design of the *Pearce Ecohouse* has been guided by my high-performance design strategy - by an interest in first principles and by my practical experience building the sophisticated architectural structures presented in the foregoing. The first principles of morphology and structural behavior that are enumerated in my book, *Structure in Nature is a Strategy for Design*, are inherent in the design of the *Pearce Ecohouse*. In addition there are other first principles that govern the form and technology of the *Ecohouse* design. These *first principles* are summarized below as they relate to the fundamental *purposes of shelters*, along with attributes that are the manifestations of these principles, and that facilitate the *Pearce Ecohouse* as an embodiment of high-performance design.

Purposes of Shelters

Climate Management

The most important and fundamental performance parameter of a shelter for human habitat, of its purpose, is the management of climate. Without this, there is no reason for a building to exist. Creating a comfortable living environment, within the resources and methods available in a given cultural and environmental setting, has been the fundamental goal of shelter design since the beginning of building. There are endless examples of this in the history of indigenous building, such as the Mesa Verde Pueblo, so beautifully described by Ralph Knowles in his valuable book, *Energy and Form*, The MIT Press, 1974.

Spatial Differentiation

As a corollary to climate management, spatial differentiation is perhaps the next most important parameter of building purpose. The differentiation of wet from dry, warm from cold, cool from hot, light from dark, quiet from noisy, public from private, view from no view, all these and more become the central considerations of shelter design at its most fundamental level.

A Sense of Well-Being

A sense of well-being is the ultimate purpose of shelter design, especially housing. This can only be achieved by first addressing *Climate Management* and *Spatial Differentiation*. It is widely held that two of the most important contributors to a *sense of well-being* are access to sunlight (natural light) and fresh air (natural ventilation). Environmental temperateness, access to view, and adaptive open space are other fundamental attributes that are also important contributors to a sense of well-being.

Longhouse Pueblo, Mesa Verde, Colorado, at mid-day in July.
At the high sun angle of summer the Pueblo is in shade during the hottest part of the day. At the lower sun angle of winter, the Pueblo is heated directly by solar radiation. A helpful degree of passive climate management is provided for this Pueblo built within a south-facing cave. The *Pearce Ecohouse* draws inspiration from this site built approximately 900 years ago by indigenous Americans.

Section through Mesa Verde Longhouse Pueblo settlement, from the West:

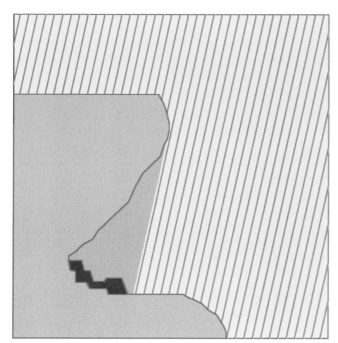

Summer sun angle.

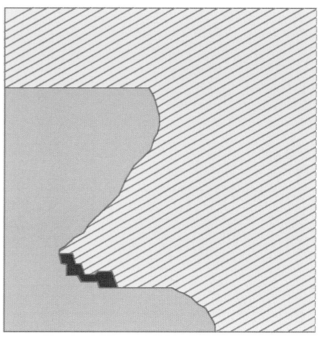

Winter sun angle.

25

Physical Principles of Climate Management

Solar Radiation: Source of Heat Gain

Solar radiation, not ambient temperature, is the primary source of heat gain. Indeed, ambient temperature is fundamentally a product of solar radiation. In warm climates, it is important to mitigate the effects of heat gain from solar radiation, and in cold climates it is important to exploit the effects of heat gain from solar radiation. In many climates where populated settlements occur, there is both the need to resist heat gain from solar radiation in the summer months, and to absorb solar radiation in the winter months.

For the purpose of maintaining a temperate environment in a warm climate, such as Southern California, the most efficient method for doing that is to intercept solar radiation before it contacts or penetrates the building envelope during the warmest months. This is a paradigm shift from conventional methods for managing heat gain, which are built around various strategies to insulate against solar radiation, or otherwise manage solar radiation.

At the same time, it is desirable to enable solar radiation to enter the building envelope during the colder winter months, which do occur in Southern California. During this period, solar radiation should not be intercepted from contacting or penetrating the building envelope.

We stated earlier that approximately half of the world's energy is consumed in the construction, operation, and maintenance of buildings. The largest operational percentage of this energy is used for cooling buildings, especially via refrigerated air conditioning. This is especially true in hot climates such as is found in Southern California. Therefore, the emphasis in the design of the *Pearce Ecohouse* is managing heat gain caused by solar radiation as the prime energy saving target.

Temperature Differential: Source of Air Movement

It is well understood that temperature differences create air movement (breezes and wind). This principle can be exploited to create cooling effects from natural ventilation, an important principle for maintaining temperate environments in warm weather without artificial mechanical cooling systems. In so doing healthy fresh air can be provided to inhabitants enhancing their sense of well-being. This can mitigate the high energy costs of cooling environments with refrigerated air conditioning. The exploitation of temperature differential as in integral principle of natural cooling is also a prime component of climate management with the *Pearce Ecohouse*.

Attributes

The core attributes for the *Pearce Ecohouse* have been directed towards the goal of sustainability, and developed around the aforementioned "first principles", "purpose of buildings", and "physical principles", and are summarized in the following:

- Net zero energy on an annualized basis.
- Passive climate management.
- Passive energy sources (photovoltaic collectors).
- Radiant heating and cooling with geothermal heat exchange.
- Abundant natural ventilation.
- Access to abundant daylight.
- Minimum site intervention – zero grading.
- Preservation of native habitat.
- High strength to weight structural system.
- Minimized enclosed surface to contained volume.
- Airtight building envelope.
- Column-free open plan for flexible use.
- Open plan for enhanced natural ventilation.
- Integrated product systems.
- Prefabricated building components.
- Factory-finished building components.
- Non-combustible building components.
- Long-life building components.
- Low-maintenance building components.
- Reconfigurable building components.
- High recycled material content.
- Reusable and recyclable materials.

Architecture

Environmentally Friendly Architecture

The *Pearce Ecohouse* develops an entire architecture around the principle of maintaining a temperate, user friendly, environment through passive management of the regional climate. This project is designed to achieve its programmatic goals with the lowest possible energy cost over time, and to minimize or eliminate the need to use depletable sources of energy for heating, cooling, and lighting. This results in net zero energy use on an annualized basis. It is also designed to use materials of construction as efficiently as possible through material selection, structure design, and building form. The building program embraces the classical architectural attributes of access to daylight, natural ventilation, temperateness, open space, and views, which promise a sense of well-being for the residents.

Design Simplicity

An open plan for the building enclosure is responsive to the preference for adaptable space, and design simplicity, which also supports the goal of material efficiency. This open plan approach to building form also minimizes surface to volume, which reduces material cost and has thermal advantages with respect to heat transfer and natural ventilation. Typical houses are designed as a collection of rooms given by the architectural program, which tend to define the building form. The open plan of the *Pearce Ecohouse* can be adapted to varied and changing spatial requirements by means of a modular storage wall system. In this way building form can be governed by optimized enclosure performance rather than preconceived room volumes.

Solar Power

Electrical power for operating the residence will be provided by an array of photovoltaic solar collectors integrated with the roof of a detached utility structure remote from the residence. In addition, there will be an array of solar thermal collector panels to provide hot water for domestic use, also integrated onto the roof of this utility structure. The utility space will function as a garage and site for the energy infrastructure. This will include inverters, and battery systems for the PV collectors, as well as a hot water storage tank.

Minimum Site Intervention

The building form is responsive to the site as its design not only reflects the opportunities for magnificent views (in all directions), but also fundamentally incorporates the existing geological and topological conditions as a primary design determinant. Minimum site intervention is an important aspect of this strategy. This means to configure, orient, position and support the house in such a way that zero grading, cutting, and filling is required. In this way the existing topography is preserved in its original state as much as possible.

Preservation of Native Plants

Consistent with minimum site intervention is the preservation of the native plants that dominate the site. Since the site is a previously undeveloped location in the Santa Monica Mountains, Los Angeles County, elevation 2200 feet, it is populated by magnificent flowering native plants, which are drought tolerant. Because such drought tolerant plants are considered a fire hazard to human settlement, there is the need and County requirement to clear brush and reduce the density of plant coverage of the site. This is done in a respectful and sensitive manner, which enhances the beauty and safety of the native plants. Many of them comprise small trees, which emerge from shrubs when brush is cleared and density is reduced. This emergence is enhanced by a process known as "lollipopping" or "raising" the shrubs/trees, by pruning the ground-hovering lower branches. This strategy preserves the ecosystem for the animals, birds, and insects that find their home in the Santa Monica Mountains, and maintains good fire and erosion control.

Serving Needs of Residents

The house is designed to serve the needs of this author and his wife. In addition to serving as a residence, the building must function as a facility for professional activity. I am able to focus on product design and architectural projects, which often involves physical models and prototypes. Therefore, the building must provide appropriate workspace. In addition, Susan Pearce is a consultant who also requires appropriate office space.

Metaphorical Barn

The architectural solution envisioned is inspired by barns and lofts that have been adapted to residential living. Large open spaces of flexible use are deemed preferable. In this case, the inspiration of the barn is mostly metaphorical. There is no interest in imitating the appearance or materials of the barn.

Design Vocabulary

The *Pearce Ecohouse* is a unique architectural solution that is developed around a design vocabulary that is distinct from traditional barn or residential construction. It is a vocabulary that has emerged from both theoretical studies, (see: *Structure in Nature is a Strategy for Design*, The MIT Press, 1978, 1990, Peter Pearce), and considerable practical experience in the design, engineering, and construction of advanced building systems. These include sophisticated space-trusses (mostly of steel), and innovative glazing and cladding systems. Perhaps the most well known of these projects is the previously mentioned Biosphere 2, in Arizona.

Form as an Agent of Performance

Building form is driven by a number a variables, beyond simply the preferences for a large column-free open space. Guided by our first principles, building form is a manifestation of the integration of form, structure, materials, and process. The *Pearce Ecohouse* truly exhibits *building form as an agent of performance.* Although it may not appear so upon first seeing the *Pearce Ecohouse*, its design is fundamentally simple. Its form minimizes surface to volume, which has thermal advantages, and reduces cost, and its structural system is assembled from a minimum number of simple-to-produce component types.

Strength of Geometry

The building shape is also designed for maximum structural advantage. The shape is guided by the concept of *strength of geometry*. In this concept, the dominant parameter for structural engineering is building shape, not strength of materials. Although necessary, strength of materials is considered a second order engineering parameter. In this design strategy magnitude and direction of forces in structural members are managed and optimized through structural form. This approach results in structural configurations that are highly efficient in terms of strength-to-weight, and can offer great resistance to any foreseeable lateral loads from earthquakes or wind. The form of the *Pearce Ecohouse* is designed according to this principle, resulting in a structure of high strength and low material weight.

Accommodating Climate Parameters

The building shape is also designed to facilitate water drainage from the roof. A stepped roof configuration is configured to assure effective water drainage, while enhancing structural strength. Building form is also configured to provide optimized advantage for other climate parameters, such as wind loads.

Beyond Prefab

Renewed Interest

Recently there has been a renewed interest in prefabrication as a method of manufacturing residential buildings. The parlance "prefab" is used to describe a variety of methods of manufacturing and construction. These include factory assembled spatial volumes, comprising segments of houses, which are then combined in assemblies at the final home site. These are generally referred to as "modular homes". Other approaches include framework and panelized systems, which are assembled into sub-sections off-site, then joined into a completed house at the home site. Alternatively, such systems may be shipped to the home site as components that are assembled into a complete house at the home site.

Building Materials

In general, prefab home construction methods tend to rely on conventional building materials, and are, for most part, based on orthogonal geometries. Although some of the prefab systems profess "green design", this seems to be fairly limited in scope. Many prefab home solutions have merit, and some offer a level of "modernist" design sophistication. However, truly high-performance design is not in evidence. Sophisticated levels of climate management, energy efficiency, low maintenance requirements, and the use of high performance/long life materials are not generally found in the prefab realm.

Building Components

The *Pearce Ecohouse* goes beyond prefab in its use of manufactured materials and the design of its building components. This will be increasingly apparent as this document unfolds. The *Pearce Ecohouse* also demonstrates climate management principles that go way beyond typical approaches found in the prefab home "industry".

Structure, Materials, and Process

Material Attributes

Material choices are not drawn from conventional construction methods, or commonly heralded *Green Building* material lists. Choices are made based on material properties appropriate for specific functions and performance objectives. Such material properties include high structural performance, specific thermal properties, high recycled content, long life, recyclability, non-combustibility, and compatibility with efficient mechanized manufacturing processes. Cost effectiveness is, of course, also an important variable. This variable is treated with respect to life cycle cost, value added, low maintenance, and long-life. Cheapest initial cost is not the primary driver, although preliminary cost analysis suggests that construction costs are comparable to conventional high-quality building methods.

Prefabricated Components

All building materials are prefabricated, pre-finished factory-made components, and all materials are fire-proof (non-combustible). No finishing, painting, fabrication, or other processes are done at the job site. The primary function at the job site is the assembly of a kit-of-parts, the assembly of which does not require the use of conventional building tradesmen.

The 80/20 Phenomenon

In the case of typical residential building in the USA the cost of construction is roughly 80% labor and 20% materials. With the *Pearce Ecohouse* it is the opposite, where material cost is 80% and labor is 20%. This is because of the higher quality long-life materials used in the *Pearce Ecohouse* compared to conventional building, and because the assembly is more efficient with respect to labor time and costs. The manufactured components are built to very high dimensional tolerances and are designed for ease and simplicity of assembly.

Low angle view from the east showing the upper and lower levels of the complex supported by concrete piers.

A view of the complex, showing a cutaway of the main structure exposing the furnished interiors of the upper and lower levels.

A cutaway view of the main structure showing the space-truss exoskeleton, and the upper and lower decks. On the left can be seen one of the space-truss buttresses supporting the upper deck from the lower deck.

Steel Strut Components

The building super-structure is made from specially designed steel strut components assembled into a three dimensional space-truss of very high strength to weight, capable of forming a large column free space, and clear span floor structure. A minimum number of strut types are required. Steel strut components are finished with a high-performance polymer coating to ensure low maintenance and long life.

Exoskeleton

The building space-truss super-structure forms an exoskeleton, which supports and is outboard of the building enclosure. The building enclosure forms a column-free "one-room" space with a floor area of 3138 square feet. The exoskeleton takes the form of a stepped geometry, which provides added strength to the clear span space-truss. As mentioned above, this configuration also facilitates roof drainage, as the enclosure shape follows the geometry of the stepped exoskeleton.

Space-truss Deck

The exoskeleton, being outboard of the building enclosure, is supported from the upper level deck, which is an extension of a space-truss which forms the floor plane of the primary living space. The exoskeleton springs directly from this deck from three zones, displaced on alternating edges of an elongated hexagonal plan form. Three space-truss buttresses support the overhead exoskeleton, and form planes that are parallel to the three faces of a triangular pyramid – a regular tetrahedron. The total deck area is 5874 square feet. It is possible to walk around the entire building enclosure from the exterior zone of the deck. The upper level space-truss deck is supported from the lower space-truss deck by three space-truss buttresses. Much like as with the exoskeleton support, these buttresses are positioned on opposite sides of the lower deck. The lower deck is elevated from the ground by the support piers, and forms the lower level space.

Interior Floor System

The interior space-truss deck/floor structure is clad with a composite floor system comprised of a cast aluminum support panel clad with a synthetic stone top panel. The aluminum support panels are attached directly to the space-truss joints via special cast spiders.

This floor system provides for thermal mass, location of hydronic tubing for radiant heating and cooling, vibration damping, high structural performance, and long life. The aluminum casting is designed to directly contain and support the hydronic tubing. In effect, the hydronic tubing is embedded directly in the aluminum casting, which is an excellent conductor of heat. The warmth (or coolness) is then transferred to the aluminum casting, which then becomes a radiator with high surface area. This becomes an efficient agent for the transfer heat or cold to the upper synthetic stone floor panel to warm or cool the enclosed space.

Temperature regulation for the radiant heating and cooling system is controlled by a heat pump, and water temperature is stabilized by geothermal heat exchange.

The composite floor panels are in the form of equilateral triangles approximately four feet on a side. The composite assembly is 4 inches thick, including the aluminum casting support component and the stone floor panel. The finish of the floor will be integral to the stone panel in the form of a polished surface.

Electrical and Network Distribution

Between the triangular panel sides are channels with removable covers, which contain electrical and network cables for distribution throughout the house.

Exterior Floor System

The exterior floor system is an all cast aluminum panel system providing cladding for all the exterior deck planes. This includes the exterior decks surrounding the interior spaces of the upper and lower levels of the residential interiors, and an access and parking deck. This deck cladding system provides for water drainage as an integral feature of its design and will accommodate rain water storage.

36

View of upper level of residence from above with supporting exoskeleton removed, showing the all glass building enclosure.

Glass Enclosure

The building enclosure is comprised entirely of insulated glass, including all exterior walls, doors, and roof. In the upper level, there are 96 operable windows around the entire vertical perimeter walls of the enclosure, and 48 operable windows in the overhead (roof) glazing. A large (3138 sq. ft.) open plan is formed with 360 degrees of view, including the ocean on the south, and the sky towards the north, with an interior washed in natural reflected (indirect) light.

In the lower level there are 82 operable windows around the entire vertical perimeter walls of the enclosed space. Of course, since this level is below the upper level, there is no overhead glass roof.

Glazing Panels

Glazing panels will be assembled, ready to install, in a shop facility under strict quality assurance through rigorous process management. When these pre-glazed panels are delivered to the site, they will be bolted into place. A site-applied silicone caulking will provide the final weather seal. The glazing system is a flush structural silicone design, including the operable windows. Such a system simplifies cleaning and minimizes thermal transfer through the glazed enclosure, since a minimum amount of metal is exposed to the outside weather.

Virtually Airtight

This glazing system will also be virtually airtight, which prevents heat loss through air leakage during the cold winter months. The amount of fresh air entering the building enclosure is controlled through the operable windows.

Outboard Sprinkler System

An outboard sprinkler system is provided to clean the exterior of the building exoskeleton and the glass enclosure. The sprinkler system will also afford protection against fires, since, as was noted in earlier, the house is located in a Southern California fire area.

Concrete Piers

The building is anchored to the terrain via twenty cast-in-place concrete piers. The piers are cast into borings of varied depth depending on soil composition, which varies over the terrain of the building site. All twenty of the piers terminate at column capitals, which are in the form of inverted hexagonal pyramids. These capitals support the space-trusses, which form the deck-floor structures. The column capitals distribute the concentrated loads from the piers into the space trusses by increasing the number of interface connection points. This divides the concentrated loads from the piers by a factor of six, since there are six connection points to the space truss from each column capital.

The strategy of supporting the *Pearce Ecohouse* project with piers enables the building to adapt to complex topography without the need for cutting and filling at the site. This eliminates the need for any grading and enables minimum site intervention. The pier support system, in combination with the high performance space-truss structural system, ensures maximum effectiveness in resisting large seismic and wind forces.

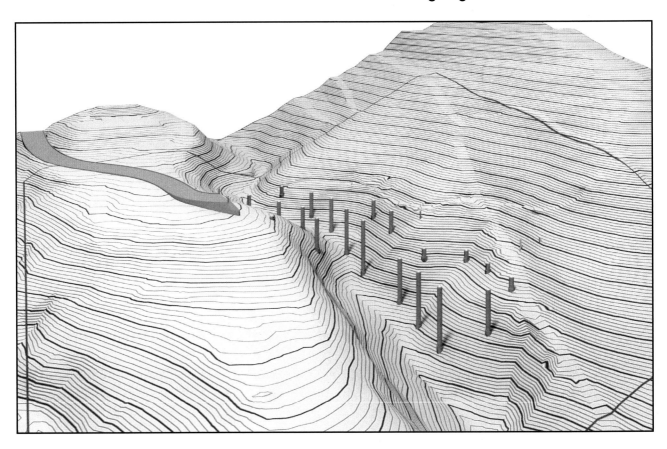

38

Architecture as Product Design

Factory Made

This is a project that is truly architecture as product design. There will be no "off-the-shelf" components used in the construction of this building. It will consist of a "kit-of-parts" that will be entirely pre-designed, pre-engineered, pre-fabricated, and pre-finished. All components, save for some fasteners, are being designed specifically and uniquely for this building application. No fabrication, cutting, welding, or painting, will be done at the job site. The factory-made components will be simply assembled at the building site. There will be no scrap generated at the site to clean up, and there will be a minimum amount of trash, limited to packing materials. There will be no details left to chance - no surprises at the project site at the time of construction (assembly). The only "conventional" building trade will be silicone caulking for the final weather seal. This project is a bit like designing and building an airplane, with every detail worked out in advance of final production. Like all product development, the first *Pearce Ecohouse* can be considered a prototype.

Design Processing

All components are being developed through the use of Computer Aided Design software. Product viability is established through the construction of full scale mock-ups created from digital files driving "rapid prototype" technology, such as "3-D Printing". With this technology components can be assembled in real space and time to verify their function. These become proof of concept methodologies that enable design intent to be perfected. Once component design is validated through rapid prototyping, tooling can be made for manufacturing from the same digital file embodiments of the "kit-of-parts".

Structural analysis is also performed with computer based engineering programs. In this way structural performance can be verified prior to construction.

Climate Management Strategies

No Air Conditioning Required

Since this residence is designed to be built in Southern California, the climate management focus is on maintaining a comfortable living environment in the hottest months, and to do so without the use of refrigerated air conditioning. It is obvious that the habitual use of refrigerated air conditioning in our culture represents a huge drain on energy consumption. Therefore, it is considered a major objective to avoid the need for refrigerated air conditioning. The *Pearce Ecohouse* is designed so there is no need to use depletable sources of energy to maintain a comfortable living environment.

Intercepting Solar Heat Gain

As was previously mentioned the primary source of discomfort from overheating is solar radiation, not ambient temperature. The outboard louvers, mounted in the exoskeleton of the *Pearce Ecohouse,* intercept solar radiation, eliminating heat gain directly from the sun on the building envelope, during the warmest months of the year (at the high sun angles). Solar radiation is intercepted before actually contacting the building surface. We call this exoskeleton, populated by louvers, a *Climate Management Canopy.* This is analogous to building a house completely under a very large tree.

 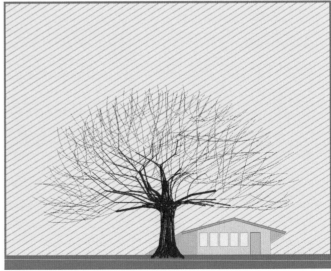

Solar radiation is blocked from warming the house under the tree in the summer (left), and, if the tree is deciduous, solar radiation will warm the house in the winter (right).

Capturing Solar Heat Gain

In the winter months at the lower sun angles, the *Climate Management Canopy* allows solar radiation to enter the building enclosure (from the south). This creates heat gain, which warms the interior. The heat is stored in the synthetic stone floor modules. Fixed louvers can be used because of the changing sun angles. The geometry of the louver system is designed specifically to achieve the interception of solar radiation in the hot months, and to enable penetration of sunlight in the cold months.

Orientation

Note that the orientation of the house is exactly on the north/south axis, and its plan form is symmetrical about this axis. This enables the predictable management of solar impact on the building.

Thermal Mass

Thermal mass provides for daily solar heat storage during winter months in the floor system. A thermal break is provided between the interior and exterior floor surfaces. This is desirable in the warm months, since the outer deck surface is prevented from transferring accumulated heat, gained from solar radiation and ambient temperature, to the interior. The reverse is true in the cold months.

Radiant Heating and Cooling

As previously described, a radiant heating/cooling system is provided. Because of the passive climate management attributes of the *Pearce Ecohouse* it is anticipated that this system will not see intensive operation for most of the year in Southern California. During the hot summer months, cooling effects are provided by coursing cool water through the same hydronic tubing that is used for heating in the winter.

Whether heating or cooling water to route through the hydronic tubing in the floors, water temperature is controlled by an electric heat pump.

Geothermal Heat Exchanger

However, before the hydronic fluid (water) is routed through the heat pump it is stabilized by a "geothermal" heat exchanger. At a predetermined depth below grade, temperature is virtually constant, in the range of plus or minus 60 degrees. There will be an underground labyrinth of hydronic tubing, in effect an underground heat exchanger, which will stabilize the water as it is pumped through, approximately matching its temperature to the ambient temperature below grade. This in turn will enable the heat pump to bring the water temperature to an optimum temperature for heating or cooling, starting with the water temperature at 60 degrees rather the from ambient air temperature.

Since the required water temperature for either heating or cooling will represent a very small gradient from 60 degrees, the heat pump will not have to use much energy. Indeed, in the case of cooling, the temperature may not require any change from the geothermal supplied water. With respect to heating, the gradient will still be very small. In short the geothermal heat exchanger principle enables very little energy to be used to power the electric heat pump. With radiant heating and cooling, temperature settings can be very moderate to achieve the desired environmental result, especially within an enclosure that is thermally efficient.

Cooling Principles

As we have stated previously, energy cost for cooling conventional buildings is very high. Therefore, in order to achieve our goal of net zero energy use on an annualized basis, the *Pearce Ecohouse* takes advantage highly energy efficient principles. Cooling of the interior is achieved and maintained through the principles of the building design, which require zero use of depletable energy sources. No mechanical air conditioning is required.

Cross ventilation is optimized by means a large number of operable windows, which are located continuously over the surface of the building's exterior walls. Combinations of windows can be selectively opened in strategic locations around the perimeter of the building enclosure to optimize the cooling effects of cross-ventilation for given conditions of the microclimate.

A large number of operable windows in the glass roof facilitate the "stack-effect", which enhances cross ventilation. These windows can be selectively opened to take best advantage of given conditions of the microclimate. The absence of conventional rooms inside the building envelope enable the airflow provided by cross-ventilation to course through the building with minimum obstruction.

The outboard louvers intercept and dissipate solar radiation, which has the effect of creating convection currents, which further draw the cooler air from the interior through the opened windows in the roof. This enhances the "stack-effect". The louvers are optimized for heat dissipation because they have high surface-to-volume. Further, they are made from aluminum extrusions, which are very effective at conducting and dissipating the heat from solar radiation.

This scheme is quite literally a form of *solar cooling*. In this scheme, air movement is generated by the temperature differential between the heated louvers and the cooler air of the shaded space under the louvers and in the building interior. The radiant cooling in the floor, using a geothermal source for cool water in the summer, adds additional cooling effects during periods of extremely hot exterior temperatures.

Insulated Glass

Insulated glass is used throughout. In combination with cellular blinds, which approximately doubles the total **U-value**, thermal transfer is mitigated. However, insulation is not considered the primary climate management tool.

Minimal Surface

Surface area of the building envelope relative to enclosed volume is minimal to optimize thermal performance. The surface area of the building enclosure is minimized, based upon the inherent simplicity of the building envelope shape, and the hexagonal derived plan form in which exterior walls meet at corners of 120° interior angles. Surface area is 6,014 square feet, and volume is 44,330 cubic feet, a ratio of .136 square feet per cubic foot (7.37 cubic feet per square foot). This low surface area geometry helps to mitigate thermal transfer between inside and out. This is particularly important during the lower outside temperatures of winter. As mentioned earlier, lower surface to volume means less building material is required, which reduces cost.

Natural Light

Because of the glass enclosure, the primary source of illumination is natural light, which is reflected and controlled by the outboard louvers. Energy is saved during daylight hours, by reducing electrical demand for artificial lighting. The heat gain that is caused by artificial lighting is also eliminated; thereby reducing cooling loads in the summer months.

The Natural Garden: Drought Tolerant Native Plants as Landscaping
The future construction site for the *Pearce Ecohouse* is a two and one half acre site with ocean view, at 2200 feet elevation in the Santa Monica Mountains. The an ocean view from the site is revealed in the image in the upper left. Note the people in the image in the lower right for a sense of the scale of the native trees.

Site Development and Landscaping

Semi-Wilderness

As noted earlier, the building site is in the Santa Monica Mountains at 2200 feet above sea level, in the County of Los Angeles. This is a semi-wilderness area comprised of low-density residential development. The building site is completely undeveloped, and is found at the end of a private road, which connects to a County road.

Mediterranean Climate

This area is characterized as a "Mediterranean climate". Such climates exhibit mild rainy winters, and hot dry summers. Within the California coastal climate there are many "microclimates" from relatively cool and damp conditions year round at the immediate coast, to very hot and dry inland regions, which can get relatively cold and wet in the winter. There are also intermediate areas that split the difference between these two extremes. The Santa Monica Mountains is one such "microclimate", where summers are not as hot as the inland valley regions but warmer than the immediate coast, and generally relatively cold in the winter. At the higher elevations, there is also a good deal more rain than is found in the lower elevations of the valleys and coastal plains.

Drought Tolerant Native Plants

The mountainous zone where the building site is found is comprised of a great variety of remarkable drought tolerant chaparral plant types. There is a vital ecosystem in the area with an impressive collection of native animals, birds, and insects, including bobcats, coyotes, mule deer, roadrunners, and an occasional mountain lion.

These plants flourish in the rainy winter and spring season, and exhibit a spectacular array of flowers, especially in the spring.

Fire Ecology

The area is also considered a fire ecology. In general, the native drought tolerant plant types are vulnerable to wild fires, as they can be highly flammable during the dry season (June through October). Outbreaks of wild fires occur especially in areas that have not seen fires for a number of years. When residential intervention occurs in the fire ecology zones, care must be taken to mitigate the danger of fires. This is accomplished in two ways. First, buildings must be constructed from non-combustible materials, and second, landscaping strategies must be implemented that repress the spread of fire.

As has been mentioned earlier, the *Pearce Ecohouse* will be entirely constructed of non-combustible materials - steel, aluminum, pre-cast concrete, and glass. This is not only part of a fire mitigation strategy; it is with these materials that building performance (in every aspect) is optimized.

Natural Habitat

In order to preserve that natural setting and the vital ecosystem, we have adopted a development strategy of minimum site intervention. This means preserving the native plants as the fundamental landscaping element, and minimizing grading, cutting, and filling. The goal is to preserve the existing topography as much as possible, since this is an integral part of the natural habitat. To make radical changes to the site requires a major disruption of the native plant communities, and therefore, the local ecosystem. The *Pearce Ecohouse* is designed to minimize any modification to the existing site topography.

Fire Hazard

With respect to the fire hazards associated with the native plants, the density of native plant communities must be reduced through thinning, brush clearance, and sensitive pruning, called "lollipopping" or "raising". When this is done, what often appear to be bushes and ground cover mature into beautiful small trees, which can reach heights of 15 to 20 feet, or higher in some species.

48

High Density

It is generally understood that the greatest fire hazard occurs when there is high-density of plant material, and in particularly low lying brush of one sort or another.
It is also important to avoid having plants immediately contiguous with the buildings on the site. When sensitive intervention of this sort is implemented the natural habitat is preserved, and fire danger is mitigated.

Density Reduction

The strategy outlined in the foregoing, with respect to fire mitigation, is a kind of simulation of the function of fire in the ecosystem. Fire is the ultimate density reduction and brush clearance method - an extreme version. The deliberate density reduction outlined above enables existing plants to flourish and provides room for long dormant plants to grow - seeming to come from nowhere. This is accomplished without compromising the native ecosystem.

Abusive Development

Conventional development in this area tends to be abusive of the native habitat and topography. Properties are aggressively cleared of plant communities, and topography is often radically modified. Conventional residential construction requires the infamous "building pad", which typically destroys the topography of the site. Once the property is cleared, there is the compulsion to landscape with invasive decorative plants, including trees, shrubs, and ground cover such as lawns, that are wholly inappropriate to the "Mediterranean climate". This results in the need for heavy irrigation requiring untoward amounts of water usage, in a climate that is fundamentally semi-arid.

Ecosystem Friendly

The landscaping strategy for the site of the *Pearce Ecohouse* can be thought of as a prototype for ecosystem friendly development. We hope to demonstrate that, not only will our approach preserve the natural habitat for the many species that make their home in this environment, but that the human habitat that is created will provide a sense of well-being and appreciation of nature's way.

Part 3

Visualizing the *Pearce Ecohouse*

Part 3
Visualizing the *Pearce Ecohouse*

VIsualizing the *Pearce Ecohouse*

In this section of the book we present a comprehensive collection of images of the *Pearce Ecohouse*. These include images of the structures with and without representations of the site.

In addition to perspective views of the exterior and interior of the project, images of plans, elevations, and sections are also included. Other special attributes of the *Pearce Ecohouse* are visualized and described, such as passive management of solar radiation, site construction, and modular storage walls for interior spatial organization. There are also images of interior plans, and perspective renderings showing how, in the open plan volumes, functional spaces are differentiated.

The Project Site

Located at 2200 feet above sea level, the property is located in the Santa Monica Mountains above Malibu, California. A view of the Santa Monica Bay is at hand with the city of Santa Monica, Los International Airport, Palos Verdes Peninsula, The Port of Los Angeles (on a very clear day), Catalina Island, and two other of the channel islands all within view.

The 2½ acre site is located at the end of a private road with 11 neighboring properties along the road. All properties are required by local regional codes to be at least 2½ acres.

The property is topologically complex and embodies a mix of geological properties, which includes zones of both ancient landslide and competent rock. These features comprise a design challenge that is readily met by the adaptive structural and morphological principles intrinsic to the *Pearce Ecohouse* system.

Google Earth Montages

Shown above is a Google Earth image of the region of the Santa Monica Mountain range in which the site for the *Pearce Ecohouse* is located. The Pacific Ocean can be seen in the upper left of the picture. The image is oriented with south to the left and north to the right. The view of the image is essentially from due east. A montage is created by placing a rendered image of the *Pearce Ecohouse* on the building site. The house is found just to the left of center in the lower half of the view.

Moving closer in with Google Earth, the *Pearce Ecohouse* position on the site is more discernible. Note that the house is "floating" over a mini-ravine - what the geologist calls an ephemeral ravine.

This shows the same Google Earth image, showing the extent of the actual property, overlaid Is a 3-D topological map. The property line falls within the topomap. The 2½ acre site is generally square in projected plan and is approximately 330 feet on each side of the property line.

Photomontage

Here we see a rendered image of the *Pearce Ecohouse* superimposed on an actual photograph of the site, viewed from the southwest. The landscaping is comprised entirely of native plants. In the center of the image can be seen a mini-forest of rare small costal trees knows as Redshank. Also found on the property are three varieties of Ceanothus, Laurel Sumac, Manzanita, Willow, Toyon, and Holly-leaf Cherry among other small trees and shrubs. Of course, there is a large variety of other coastal scrub flora found on the site as well.

As has been mentioned in Part 1, an important part of the design strategy is systemic adaptation to the site topology and geology. This includes minimum site intervention. The goal of this strategy is the preservation of the native habitat and the regional ecosystem. With this in mind the *Pearce Ecohouse* will be built without the need for any grading or soil export, and the major percentage of native plants occupying the site will be preserved.

57

Adaptation to Site

As has been pointed out earlier, an important goal of the *Pearce Ecohouse* design is to enable minimum site intervention, in order to preserve the native habitat. To do this requires an architectural/building solution that can adapt to the complex topography of the site. In turn this requires a building system whose form is highly adaptive while providing high performance structural attributes. The sophisticated geometry of the *Pearce Ecohouse* building system facilitates both of these attributes.

The images that follow illustrate a high level of design adaptation to the configuration of the building property. In elevation and section, the variable-height supporting piers facilitate adaptation to the elevation changes. The 60° geometry of the building system itself enables the building form to adapt to the vertical and lateral contours of the property.

Above from the southeast.

58

With aerial photo mapped to the topographic model.

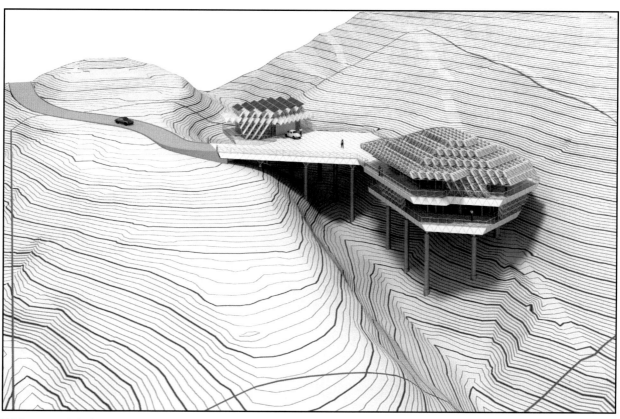

Without aerial photo showing the contour lines of the topographic model.

59

From the east an array of piers support the structure over a mini-ravine.

Piers support the lower level, while the upper level is supported by the trusses springing from three sides of the lower level. Through these trusses load is distributed between levels while providing intrinsic lateral stability.

Matching the Contours of the Building Site

The following six images illustrate the extent to which the building system enables the architecture to match the contours of the building site. The shape of the site has not been altered in any way through grading or any soil removal. The site contours are matched exactly as they have been found, untouched by any terra-forming.

These images reveal a remarkable level of spatial adaptation, not readily available using conventional approaches to residential building methods and design assumptions. These structures flow with the contours of the land without being of self-conscious or contrived form.

This level of adaptation is available through the spatial vocabulary intrinsic to the *Pearce Ecohouse* building system geometry. This is a system of a minimum number of standardized structural components out of which the entire building structure complex is assembled. These components comprise tubular steel struts joined with a simple proprietary connection system. This connection system is integral to the strut components. As has been pointed previously, it is not the mission of this document to present the development and details of these components. This story will be told in subsequent future documents.

Above from the north.

Above from the northwest.

Above from the west.

62

Above from the northeast.

Above from the northwest.

Zooming in from the northwest shows the stairways to advantage. The left side of the image reveals two stairways along the north edge of the building. One, on the left, provides access between the upper level and lower level. The second on the north side of the building provides access to the site from the lower level.

On the far right side of the image is a third stairway, which provides access from the deck to the lower level and to the property. These are the only stairways connecting the upper and lower levels of the residence. There is no internal primary stairway connecting the levels. This is to provide visual and acoustic privacy between the levels. There is a utility stairway that connects the levels that is located within corresponding service cores found in both levels. The upper service core is located directly above the lower service core. These service cores will be described in more detail later. The stairways are assembled from a system of components that are dimensionally coordinated with the structural system of the *Pearce Ecohouse.* Note that the access deck, a corner of which is seen on the right of the image, is co-planar with the upper (primary) level of the residence. The garage and general parking and vehicle turnaround is on that same level.

Walking Around the *Pearce Ecohouse*

The next series of images comprises a kind of walk-around, moving closer-in for a more intimate look at the *Pearce Ecohouse*. The architecture provides an exterior deck (porch) that extends around the entire building on both the upper and lower levels. The deck on the upper level is on the same elevation (coplanar) as the access/parking deck, and garage floor. Residents and visitors can circumnavigate the exterior of the enclosures on these decks and enjoy a variety of different views from ocean to mountains.

The interior spaces are entirely enclosed with flush mounted insulated glass panels. There are operable windows on the vertical glazing that repeat continuously on every window bay. There are additional operable glazing panels in the roof system which is 100% glazed. There are no opaque panels anywhere on the enclosures of the *Pearce Ecohouse*.

Approaching the complex from the southwest. Note the vehicle on the driveway heading toward the access deck and garage.

A sense of the scale of the building is given in this close-in view from the south. The building is clearly "floating" over the mini-ravine. One of the three truss assemblies supporting the upper level from the lower level can clearly be seen along the lower edge of the south face of the structure.

On the left, the vehicle access deck is seen at the elevation common to the floor plane of the upper residential space. The load-distributing column capitals emerging from the support piers can be seen under the access deck and lower floor level.

A sense of scale is conveyed with images of people shown at random locations on the decks. A steel strut-based railing with glass in-fill panels is provided for security. The floor space-trusses are enclosed with triangular panels to deflect wind and improve thermal performance. The decks overlook the mini-ravine, where water run-off flows during heaving rain. At such moments residents can enjoy the rhythms of a cascading stream as it meanders down the ravine. The structures are elevated from the terrain, which insures that the enclosures are not susceptible to flooding caused by occasional heavy rain.

In this image, the louver scheme provides shade in the summer from the morning sun. Note that the building form is perfectly symmetrical about a north-south symmetry plane. Because of this symmetry, the west side is the mirror opposite of the east side. Since the sun angle in the afternoon is the mirror of the sun angle in the morning a symmetrically opposite louver scheme is effective for shading on the west side as well.

Looking northwest, with access deck left.

Looking from the southeast.

Looking west from the south upper deck.

Looking west from the north upper deck.

Looking west toward the upper deck.

Looking west toward the lower level.

Looking north toward the lower level.

West stairway connecting levels.

Lower north deck, looking west.

71

Stairway from lower to upper level.

North side stairway to all levels.

Looking toward west side stairway.

North side stairway connecting upper and lower level, and connecting to grade.

Looking east under vehicular access deck toward the lower level. Column capitals perched on the piers, to distribute concentrated loads, can be readily seen.

Site Construction and Assembly

As was characterized earlier, the *Pearce Ecohouse* can be considered architecture as product design. Among other things, this means that all building components are manufactured off-site ready for assembly at the project site. It is truly a "kit-of-parts" system, requiring no conventional "trades" at the job site. There will be no cutting, welding, painting, drywall, or plastering required. All materials used are non-combustible. Component materials include steel, aluminum, glass, and synthetic stone. All materials have high-recycled content, and are recyclable. The components are also reusable and have a very high life cycle. Maintenance is minimized over many decades because of the high material quality, including finishes.

The building components are manufactured to high-tolerance, which guarantees proper fit at the time of assembly at the project site. With the *Pearce Ecohouse* material represents 80% of the building costs and labor 20% of the cost. This is approximately the reverse with conventional residential building construction, where labor is 80% and materials are 20%. With the *Pearce Ecohouse* the high quality long life materials are intrinsic to the building costs. This compares to the high maintenance materials used in conventional residential construction.

Building components will be delivered to the job site according to a "just-in-time" plan. This mean no components will be delivered to the site in advance of their need. There will be no warehousing of materials at the project site or anywhere else. Only the components that are actively needed for the immediate and ongoing assembly will be at site.

Preparation of tooling and manufacture of components will take six to nine months, while site assembly will take six to nine weeks. Site preparation is relatively minimal. There is no significant grading and no conventional foundations. The structural complex is supported from approximately 20 cast-in-place concrete piers, which require borings to various depths depending on the soil composition. The geology varies under the plan-form of the structural complex from sandy soils to mostly competent rock.

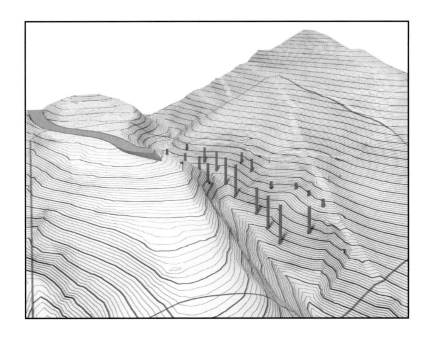

In the sequence of site construction/assembly, the first step is to bore holes for the twenty concrete piers. The grading and paving of the driveway will be done after the house is completed and all construction equipment is removed from the site.

Once the piers are set, assembly of the structures can begin. Subassemblies of the lower floor structure are built on site and lifted into position on stipulated piers and fixed in place.

The glazing enclosure for the lower level has been installed in this image, although this will actually be installed after the structural assemblies are completed. The actual next step is to assemble the three trusses that support the second level.

Subassemblies of the space trusses are constructed for the upper level floor trusses of the residence, lifted into place, and secured. The access deck and garage floor trusses are similarly constructed and lifted into place and secured. The floor deck panels are installed and the deck is used as a staging area to complete the structural assemblies of the overhead exoskeletons.

The glass enclosures for the upper level of the residence and the garage are shown, although in the construction sequence these enclosures are not installed until after the overhead exoskeletons are completed. As we have pointed out earlier, the glazing enclosures actually hang form the exoskeleton structures.

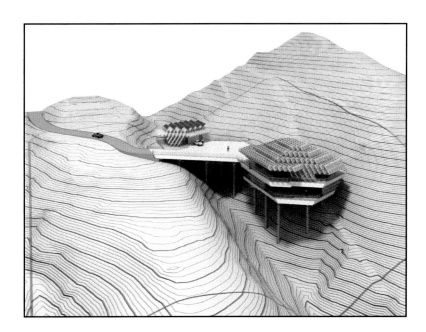

Shown is the completed *Pearce Ecohouse* complex. After the glazing enclosures are installed, the louvers and photovoltaic panels on the garage are installed.

Completing Construction

Once the assembly and installation of the structures, glazed enclosure systems, and louvers are completed there are many additional systems and functions that need to be completed before the *Pearce Ecohouse* is habitable. These include the radiant heating/cooling system, the waste management septic system, photovoltaic panels and infrastructure, electrical and networking distribution, interior furnishings, kitchen and bathrooms, and the paving of the driveway.

Photovoltaic Solar Collectors

The *Pearce Ecohouse* is entirely powered by electricity sourced from photovoltaic solar collectors. These solar panels are mounted on the garage roof structure. Within the garage is the infrastructure to harvest the power from the solar collectors. This includes inverters that convert DC to AC current and that manage power distribution to the building complex. The system will be grid interactive, which means when excess electricity is produced it will be shunted back into the public electrical grid. This happens via reversing the electric meter serving the project. When the solar panels are generating less power than what is needed at any given moment, power can be drawn from the grid. The capacity of the photovoltaic array with be sized to enable a "net zero" annual energy use from the public utility, thereby contributing zero to energy consumption.

Radiant Heating and Cooling

By way of review as earlier described, the radiant heating/cooling system is comprised of a system of hydronic tubing that courses through the floors of the building, distributing heated or cooled fluid to manage ambient temperature in the building. The fluid medium is heated or cooled via a heat pump. The fluid is cycled through a geothermal heat exchanger comprised of a labyrinth of underground pipes. Since the temperature below grade is approximately 60 degrees year round, the temperature gradient to warm or cool the hydronic fluid is minimized.

As the hydronic fluid courses through the geothermal heat exchanger its temperature is automatically adjusted to the underground temperature. This means the heat pump does not have to work very hard to manage the temperature of the hydronic fluid. Temperatures required for warming or cooling an enclosed space with radiation is much lower than with forced air. Such a system minimizes the energy load to heat and cool the building, which is already thermally efficient by design.

The installation of this geothermal heat pump system requires locating the underground pipes, installing the heat pump and distribution manifolds, and laying the hydronic tubing in the floor system. The floor system is a modular system designed to receive the hydronic tubing in a cast aluminum sub-floor that is overlaid with synthetic stone surface module. The system geometry is matched to the geometry of the space truss.

Waste Management System

The waste disposal system is a sophisticated septic system whose specifications are mandated by the Los Angeles County Department of Building and Safety. This system includes a prefabricated septic tank along with two site-constructed seepage pits. The pits require deep borings of 4 feet in diameter, and are lined with large stacked perforated concrete tubular modules.

Interior Finishing

The various requirements to complete the building to be ready to be occupied include the following: spatial differentiation using a modular storage wall system, permanently enclosed bathrooms and service cores, permanent kitchen installation, and power and networking installations.

Driveway

The driveway will be paved with tiles that offer some level of permeability for drainage. This will be one to very last items to be completed.

The Glass Enclosure

As described earlier, the building enclosure is comprised entirely of insulated glass, including all exterior walls, doors, and roof. There are 96 operable windows around the entire vertical perimeter walls of the enclosure, and 48 operable windows in the overhead (roof) glazing. A large 3138 sq. ft. open plan is formed with 360 degrees of view, including the ocean on the south, and the sky towards the north, with an interior washed in natural reflected (indirect) light. There is a total of 714 individual glazing panels in the upper level, including both fixed and operable windows.

The entire vertical perimeter walls of the lower level include 82 operable windows. All the windows in the lower level are identical to those found in the vertical walls of the upper level. There are no overhead windows in the lower level, since it is under the deck of the upper level. There is a total of 205 glazing units in the lower level including fixed and operable windows.

Glazing Panels

Glazing panels will be assembled, ready to install, in a shop facility under strict quality assurance through rigorous process management. These pre-glazed panels are comprised of insulated glass panels bonded to extruded aluminum frames with structural silicone. When these pre-glazed planes are delivered to the site, they will be bolted into place. A site-applied silicone caulking will provide the final weather seal. The glazing system is a flush structural silicone design, including the operable windows. Such a system simplifies cleaning and minimizes thermal transfer through the glazed enclosure, since a minimum amount of metal is exposed to the outside weather. This glazing system will also be virtually airtight, which prevents heat loss through air leakage during the cold winter months. The amount of fresh air entering the building enclosure is controlled through the operable windows.

Outboard Sprinkler System

An outboard sprinkler system is provided to clean the exterior of the building exoskeleton and the glass enclosure. The sprinkler system will also afford protection against fires.

Enclosure Envelope Upper Level

Shown without the supporting exoskeleton, the enclosure is comprised of 100% insulated glass with operable windows in each vertical wall segment around the perimeter, and operable windows in the glass roof. The upper level interior is revealed showing the enclosed bathrooms and utility core on the left, the kitchen in the center, and the modular storage wall system defining functional spaces.

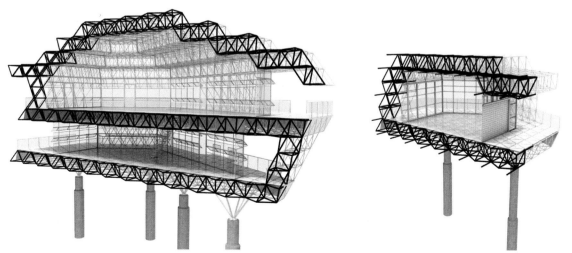

Cutaways showing the exoskeletons from which the glass enclosures are supported. The residence is shown on the left including the lower level. The garage is on the right.

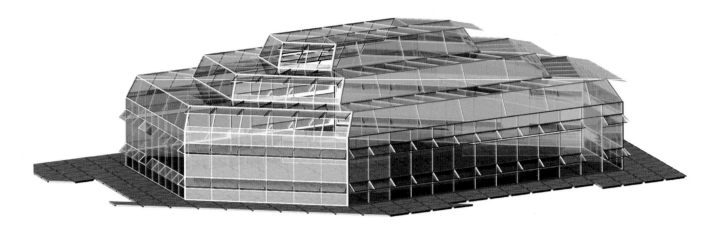

Glass enclosure of the upper level residence, without the supporting exoskeleton, showing the operable windows. The stepped geometry of the volume is designed to provide drainage from rain. There is a two degree slope designed into the nominally horizontal overhead glazing. This geometry also reflects the structural form of the exoskeleton.

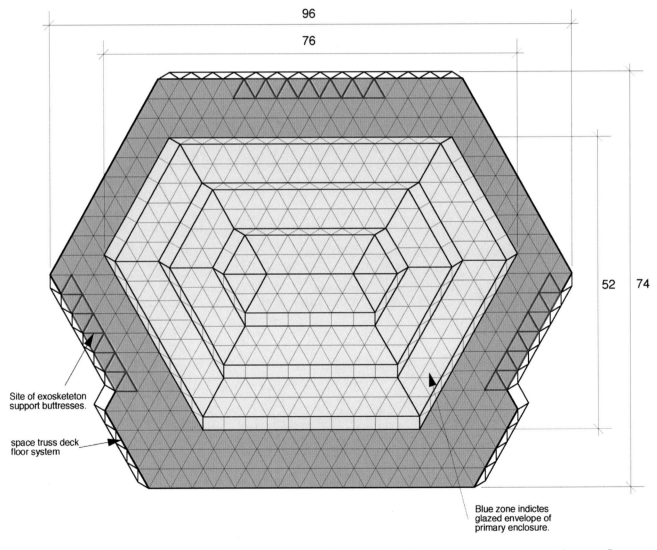

Plan view showing deck and inner chords of the exoskeletal space-truss that supports the glass enclosure. Support buttresses of exoskeleton structure are not shown, although the three zone of their interface with the floor deck are shown in red. Note that dimensions are given in feet.

N

NORTH ELEVATION

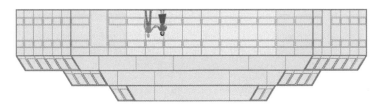

WEST ELEVATION

EAST ELEVATION

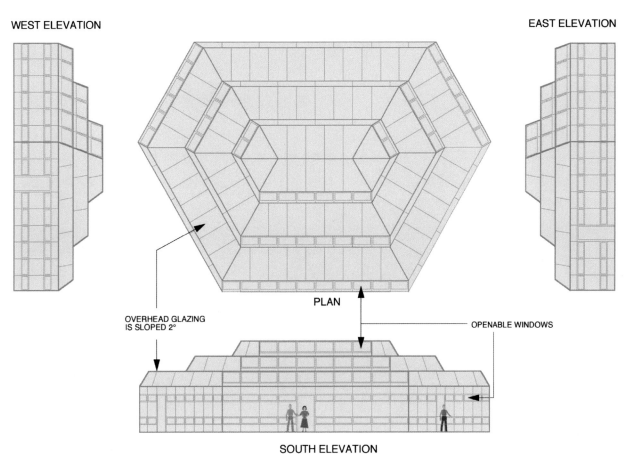

PLAN

OVERHEAD GLAZING
IS SLOPED 2°

OPENABLE WINDOWS

SOUTH ELEVATION

Plan and elevations of glass enclosure of upper level, formatted in the convention of an engineering or product design drawing. Drawings of human figures show to scale.

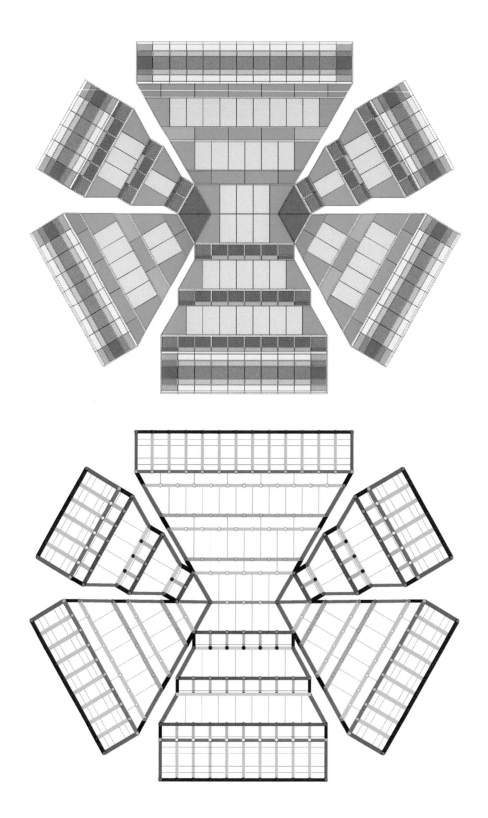

Glass enclosure is "unfolded" onto flat plane. The top image is color coded to show all of the glass panel types that are required for the upper level of the residence. There are 714 individual glazing panels required and there are 19 glazing panel types, including three panels that occur in right and left configurations. The bottom image is color coded to identify the glazing system framing components, which are aluminum extrusions. Only the upper level glazing is shown. The lower level adds no new panel types and includes 205 additional glass panels.

Climate Management Canopy

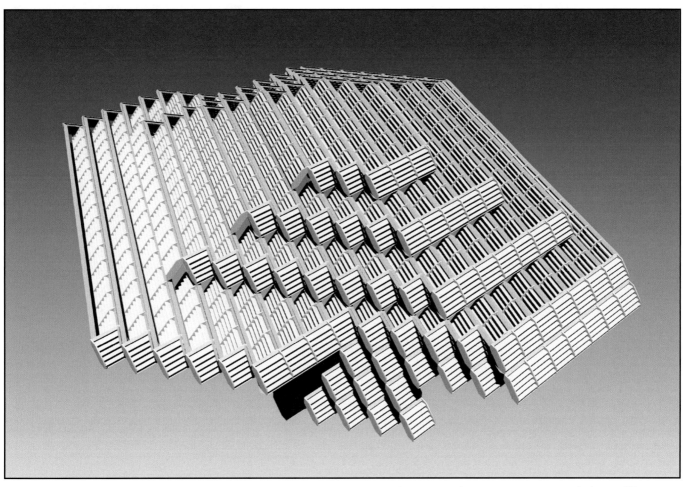

The louvers of the Climate Management Canopy are shown without the supporting space-truss exoskeleton. The view is from above looking generally in a western direction.

Overhead Louvers

Overhead louvers are mounted within the three dimensional exoskeleton. The louvers are designed to intercept and dissipate the thermal gain due to solar radiation, during the hot months of the year. In addition, indirect natural light is provided, minimizing the need for artificial light during daylight hours. During the winter months some direct sunlight is allowed to enter the building, thereby warming the interior. The louvers are manufactured from extruded aluminum and attached directly to the steel space-truss exoskeleton.

Climate Management Canopy

The effects of solar radiation through all 12 months of the year are managed by a louver scheme integrated into an exoskeleton space-truss structure. This assembly comprises a *Climate Management Canopy*, which intercepts solar radiation in the warm months preventing heat gain on the building envelope. In the colder winter months solar radiation is allowed to enter the building envelope, warming the interior.

The images shows segment of the *Climate Management Canopy*, viewed from the west as cross-sections, for each month of the year. Sun angles are shown on the 21st of each month. June 21 and December 21 are respectively summer and winter solstice. Note the sun angle reciprocity for ten of the months. These sun angles are taken at a latitude of 34 degrees north. The building enclosure hangs from and below the *Climate Management Canopy*.

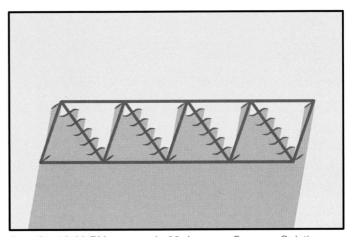

June 21, 12:00 PM, sun angle 80 degrees -Summer Solstice

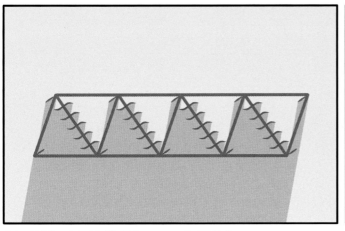

July 21/May 21, 12:00 PM, sun angle 76.5 degrees.

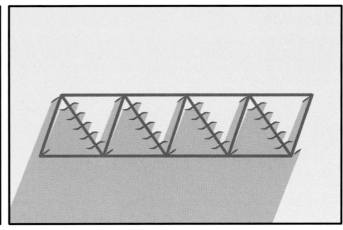

August 21/April 21, 12:00 PM, sun angle 68 degrees.

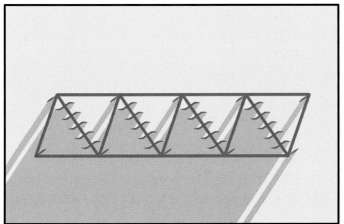

September 21/March 21, 12:00 PM, sun angle 56 degrees.

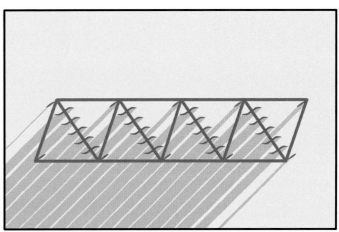

October 21/February 21, 12:00 PM, sun angle 44 degrees.

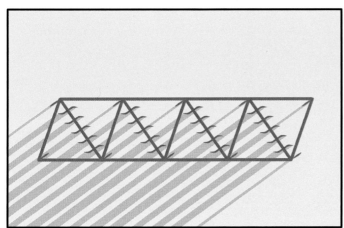

November 21/January 21, 12:00 PM, sun angle 35.5 degrees.

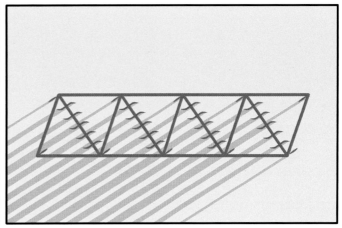

December 21,12:00 PM, sun angle 31.5 degrees -Winter Solstice

Interior Views of Solar Radiation Management

Monthly Performance: Images

The series of images shown below demonstrate the performance of the *Climate Management Canopy*, which is comprised of an outboard louver system mounted within the structural exoskeleton. This exoskeleton supports the glass enclosure of the *Pearce Ecohouse*. This demonstration is accomplished through a series of computer-generated images of the interior space of the house. These images were collected in monthly groups in which images were generated in hourly increments beginning at 7am and continuing until 5:00pm. In the present document, we show each month of the calendar year. For space considerations we have only included examples at 12:00 pm.

Note that the 21st of each month is shown, because the highest and lowest sun angles during the year occur on the 21st of June (summer solstice) and the 21st of December (winter solstice) respectively. In order to have even monthly increments; all months shown are on the 21st day. In Southern California, we have considered October 21, as a transition date from warm months to cool months from the point of view of sun angles.

The computer program, in this case *form·Z*, can position the light (a simulated sun) according to the time of day, calendar day, and the global location: latitude = 34° (e.g. Los Angeles). In so doing it is possible to see exactly when, where, and how much sunlight (if any) is allowed to enter the enclosed space. In this way it is possible to understand the performance of the louver system in managing the effects of sunlight on the enclosed space.

Two versions of the computer model have been generated. One is a perspective view from the northeast and the other is a plan view.

The perspective view looks into the interior from the north-northeast. A section has been taken just inside the plane of the exterior glass wall normal to north-northeast direction of view. This procedure removes all components, which reside on the outboard (east) side of the plane defined by the section. This enables an unobstructed view into the interior, and shows a cut or section through the floor, louvers, strut components, and other components that occur in the plane of the section. The lower utility space can barely be seen in the lower part of the image (under the floor level) but falls entirely inside the section plane.

The plan view looks into the interior from overhead - a view in plan. A section has been taken parallel to the floor, which cuts through the vertical glazed walls of the enclosure. This procedure removes all components, which reside above the plane defined by this section. This enables an unobstructed view into the interior so that patterns of solar leakage and shade can be observed normal to the floor plane of the building interior.

In spite of the fact that a clear view of the interior is enabled the light source (simulated sun) does not recognize these cuts. Shadowing occurs as if the cut has not occurred. The light source recognizes all components on both sides of the section planes. In this way the effects of daily and seasonal solar trajectories on the building envelope are accurately represented, while at the same time a clear view into the interior is enabled.

Note that in these computer models all of the glazing mullions are included but the actual glass has been deleted from the rendering. It was found that when simulated glass is included in the model it blocks the accurate generation of solar leaks. This in turn leads to unreliable images relative to solar radiation management by the louver design scheme.

The general principle of climate management for the *Pearce Ecohouse* is to intercept solar radiation during the warm months before it contacts or enters the enclosed space, and to allow solar radiation to enter the enclosed space in the cool months. It is, in effect, a simulation of a deciduous shade tree, which is opaque to the sun in the warm months and transparent to the sun in the cool months.

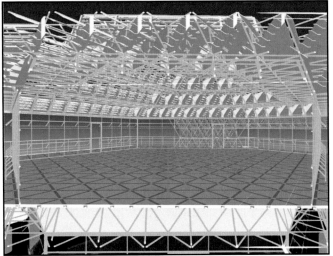

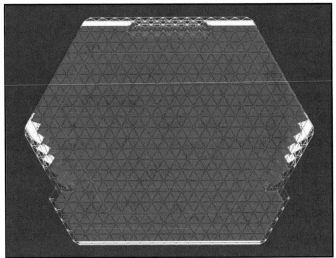

Interior Cutaway from East Northeast   Plan View of Upper Level Floor

JUNE 21, at 12:00 pm: These images show that solar radiation is completely intercepted.

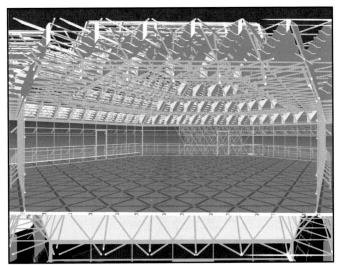

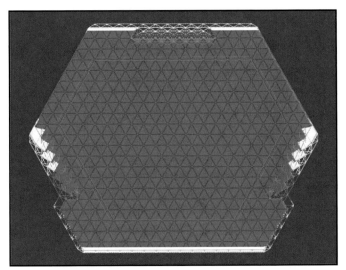

Interior Cutaway from East Northeast   Plan View of Upper Level Floor

MAY/JULY 21, at 12:00 pm: These images show that solar radiation is completely intercepted.

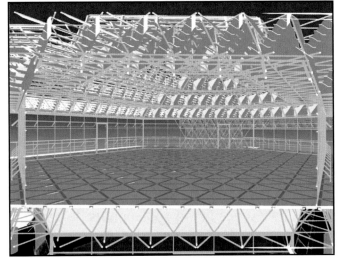

Interior Cutaway from East Northeast   Plan View of Upper Level Floor

APRIL/AUGUST 21, at 12:00 pm: These images show that solar radiation is completely intercepted.

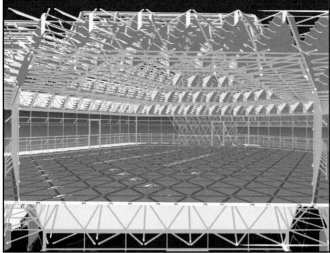

Interior Cutaway from East Northeast

Plan View of Upper Level Floor

MARCH/SEPTEMBER 21, at 12:00 pm: Images show solar radiation is virtually completely intercepted.

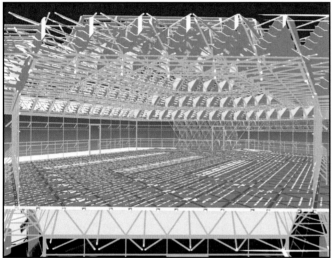

Interior Cutaway from East Northeast

Plan View of Upper Level Floor

FEBRUARY/OCTOBER 21, at 12:00 pm: Solar radiation is beginning to penetrates the building envelope.

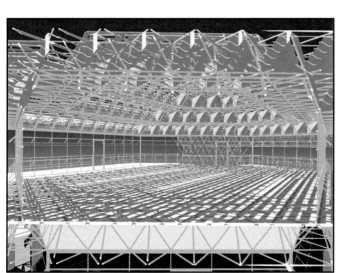

Interior Cutaway from East Northeast

Plan View of Upper Level Floor

JANUARY/NOVEMBER 21, at 12:00 pm: Showing that solar radiation penetrates the building envelope.

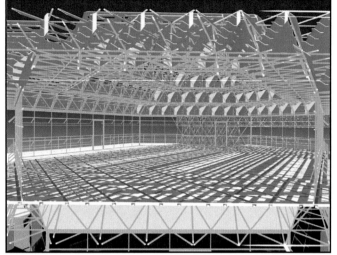

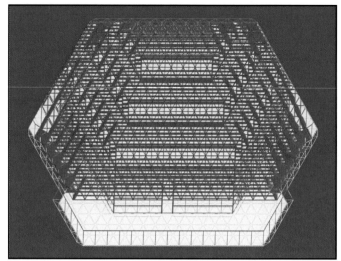

Interior Cutaway from East Northeast
Plan View of Upper Level Floor
DECEMBER 21, at 12:00 pm: Showing that solar radiation penetrates the building envelope.

With the *Climate Management Canopy* solar radiation never contacts the building enclosure in the hot months, thereby eliminating heat gain caused by solar radiation, the primary source of temperature increase. During the cool months the solar radiation enters the building enclosure, thereby warming the space.

The exoskeleton, which supports a glass building enclosure, contains a system of fixed louvers. In the interest of technical simplicity and minimizing expense, the use of fixed louvers is considered appropriate. With the use of fixed louvers it is not possible to perfectly manage solar radiation results. However, the added complexity of moveable louvers does not offer enough performance improvement to justify the added cost, especially in the relatively mild climate of Southern California. If we were to build such a climate management scheme in a more northern latitude, moveable louvers would be required for the louver scheme to be fully effective.

Using fixed louvers, a compromise solution enables this passive system to manage solar radiation with remarkable effectiveness. The images in this document illustrate this fact. In the warmer months the interior space is entirely in shade, because solar radiation is intercepted by the louver system. In the cooler months solar radiation entering the building enclosure can be observed as the brighter zones on the floor surface of the interior. These can be thought of as solar leaks, which are desirable in the winter months, but not in the summer months.

Note that at the extreme sun angles that occur in the early morning (7:00am), and late afternoon (5:00pm), a small amount of solar leakage can be detected in the warmer months. At such low angles of incidence heat gain due to solar radiation is weak, and since the area of leakage is of such small area, this does not represent a significant problem. Also, in the warm months this solar leakage is of very short duration. In the cooler months such early and late hour solar leakage is welcome even though at those hours it is weak.

Below, a chart of Sun Angle Reciprocities has been included. Shown are both daily and monthly reciprocities. With respect to daily reciprocities the sun angles in the morning comprise (approximately) the mirror images of the sun angles in the afternoon. As an example the sun angle at 2:00pm is the mirror image of the sun angle at 10:00am. This means that the pattern of solar leaks (when they occur in the cool months) will be (approximately) the same at 2:00pm and 10:00am, but in opposed symmetry.

Sun Angle Reciprocities

Time of Day Reciprocities			Monthly Reciprocities		
AM	equals	PM			
6:00	equals	6:00	December	equals	December
6:30	equals	5:30	January	equals	November
7:00	equals	5:00	February	equals	October
7:30	equals	4:30	March	equals	September
8:00	equals	4:00	April	equals	August
8:30	equals	3:30	May	equals	July
9:00	equals	3:00	June	equals	June
9:30	equals	2:30			
10:00	equals	2:00			
10:30	equals	1:30			
11:00	equals	1:00			
11:30	equals	12:30			
12:00	equals	12:00			

Regarding the monthly reciprocals, since January and November comprise the same sun angles through the course of the day, it is not necessary to look at both months. However, these monthly reciprocities reveal the need for a compromise in climate management performance when using fixed louvers. Specifically, in Southern California, reciprocal months such as October and February have distinctly different climatic conditions. Where February is a relatively cold month, often with stormy weather, early October can be quite hot.

A similar conflict exists between March and September, the latter being one of the hottest months of the year in Southern California. As mentioned earlier, October 21 is considered a transition date from warm climate to cooler climate in Southern California. The strategy of louver design was to hold back solar leakage until after October 21. At which point, heading into fall and winter, solar leakage begins to dramatically increase in order to contribute warmth in the interior of the *Pearce Ecohouse*.

Even in the cold months Southern California is a mild climate. However, the higher ambient temperatures of September and early October represent more of a concern than the colder temperatures of February and March. Similar conflicts exist between April and August, and May and July, although to a lesser degree.

In Southern California managing overheating through conventional methods (e.g. air conditioning) is very energy intensive. Since the *Pearce Ecohouse* is intended to manage climate without resorting to the use of conventional air conditioning (and heating), the louver design scheme has been configured to optimize performance for the hottest months.

Although there will be radiant heating and cooling provided in the residence, the goal is to minimize the extent of its use. The *Climate Management* strategy supports this objective.

Project Plans, Elevations, Sections, Views

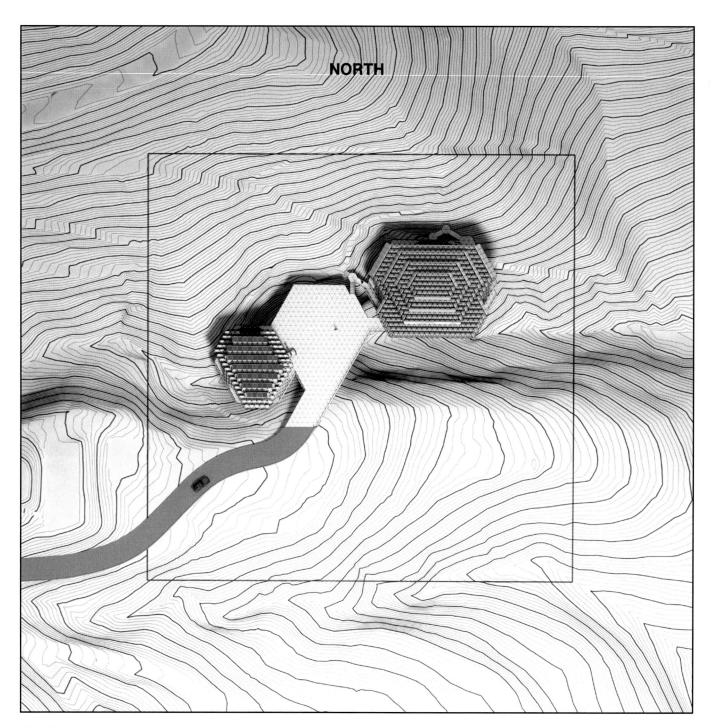

Site Plan for *Pearce Ecohouse*
Site is approximately 320 feet square in plan comprising 2.5 acres. The roof of the garage supports photovoltaic and solar thermal collectors. Inside the garage are the energy infrastructure components including inverter/ transformers and battery storage. Floor area of the garage is 1217 square feet. A limited amount of grading is required for the driveway, which matches the contour of the terrain. As has been shown earlier, the garage, access deck, and residence are supported from piers that adapt these structures to the contour of the terrain. Minimizing site intervention is thus achieved. The site is populated with many small drought tolerant native trees and shrubs, and has an ocean view from an average elevation of 2200 feet.

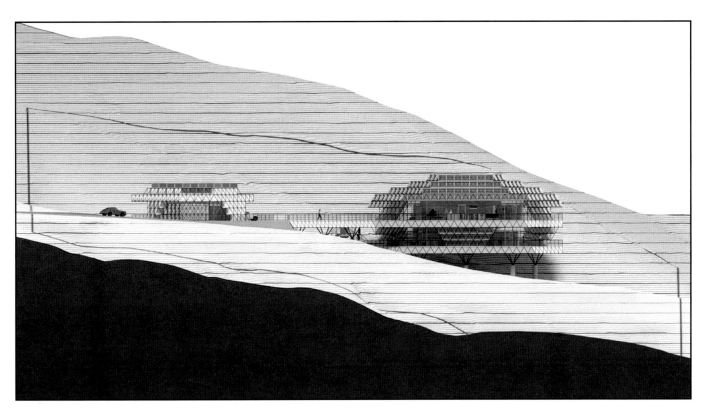

South Elevation: Showing the *Pearce Ecohouse* complex recessed into the topography of the site over the "ephemeral ravine".

Photograph of the actual site from the south, with a computer generated rendering superimposed into the image. The native plants, consisting of many drought tolerant small trees, dominate the landscape. The buildings are fully integrated into this landscape.

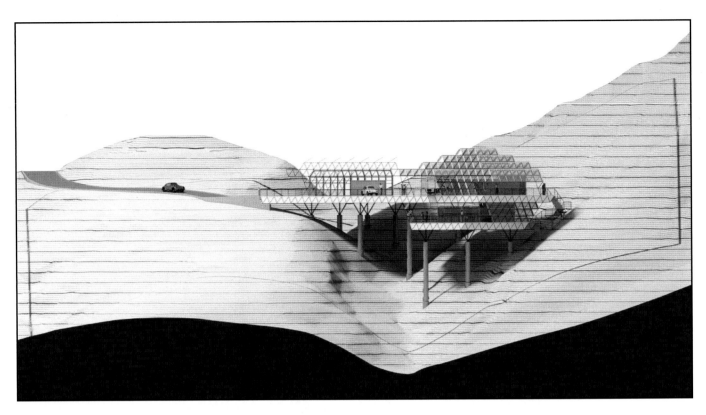

East Elevation:
Showing structures adapted to the topography of the site.

North Elevation:
Since the north property line is at a higher elevation than that of the highest point on the structure, the foreground is really a section taken just north of the structures. A cut through the site at the elevation of the north property line would completely block a view of the structures.

West Elevation:
The foreground section is taken approximately at the western property line.

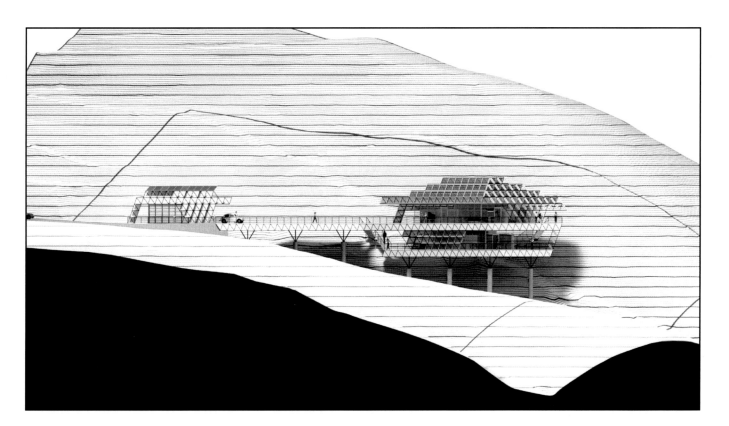

Southeast Elevation

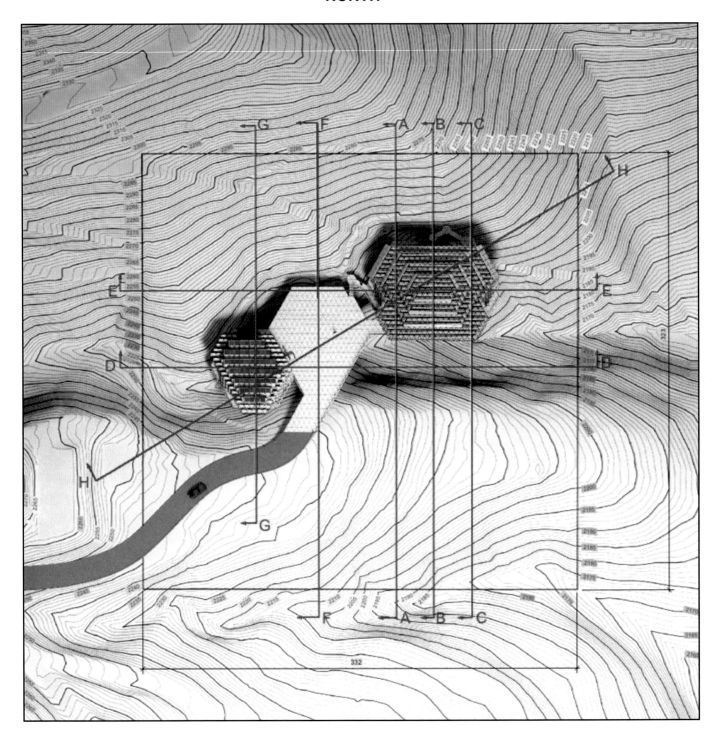

Site Plan with Sections
The site sections indicated above of the *Pearce Ecohouse* property are shown in the following images.

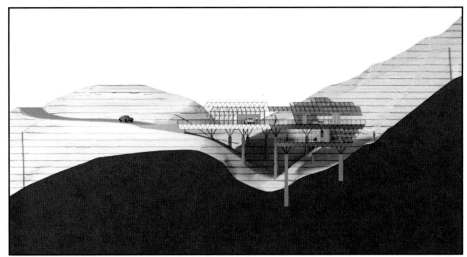

Section A-A: from the east

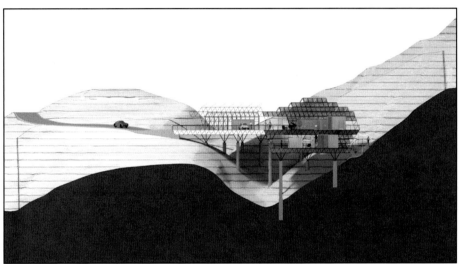

Section B-B: from the east

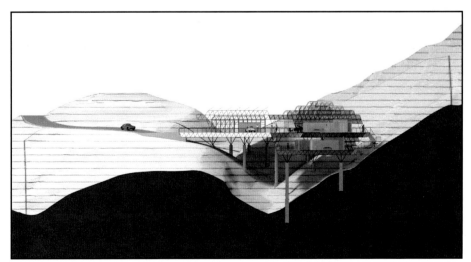

Section C-C: from the east

Section D-D: from the south

Section E-E: from the south

Section F-F: from the east

Section G-G: from the east

Section H-H: from the southeast

103

NORTH

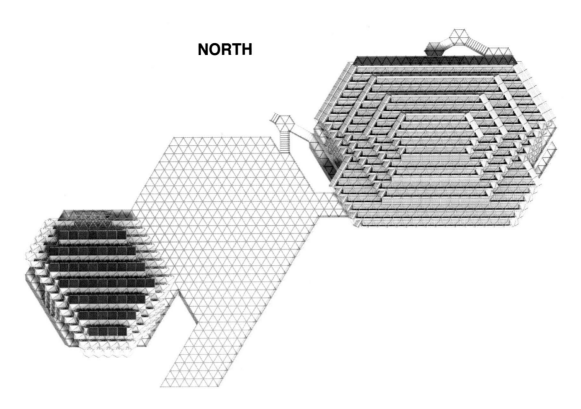

Plan view of the *Pearce Ecohouse* complex with the site not shown. Note the stairways providing access between levels and to grade. The photovoltaics can be readily seen on the roof of the garage (left side of image).

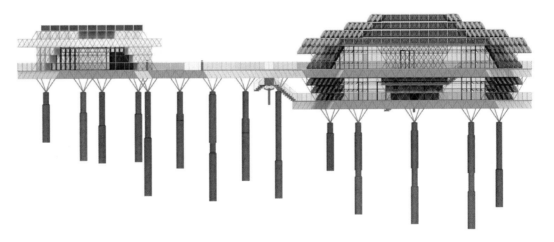

South elevation of the complex with the site not shown, revealing the piers of various lengths supporting the structures. Inverted column capital pyramids are clearly shown atop each pier. Since these capitals are hexagonal pyramids they serve to distribute the concentrated loads from the piers to six space truss connections. This means that concentrated loads transferred into the space truss are reduced by a factor of six, than if the piers were joined directly to the space truss floor structures. Note that in this view the complex is exactly 220 feet wide at its maximum extent.

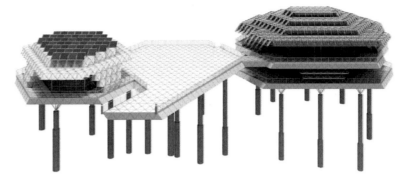

View from South

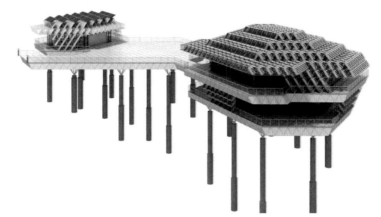

View from Southeast

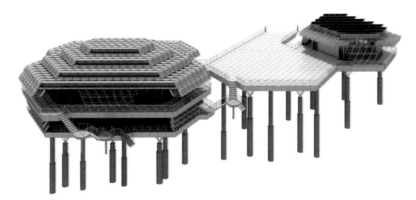

View from North

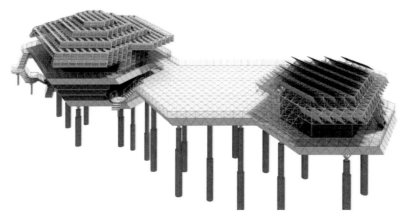

View from Northwest

Residence Plan

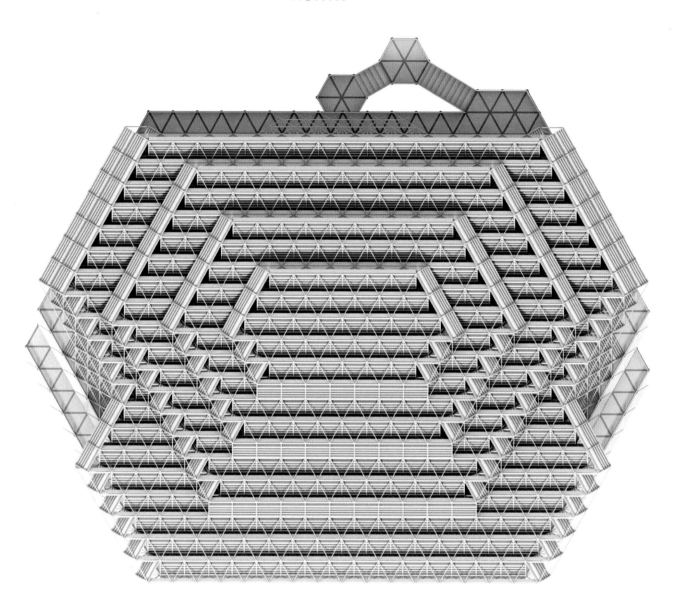

Plan view of the residence only, showing the exoskeleton populated by the louver system. Note the mirror symmetry of the structure about the north/south plane ignoring the stairway on the north side of the building.

Residence Views

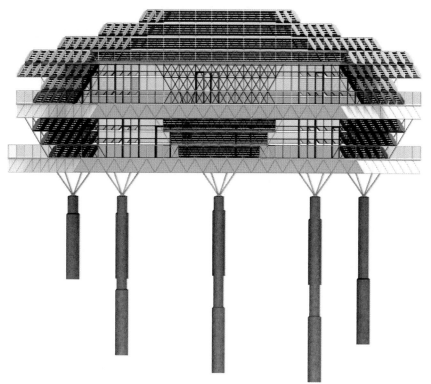

South elevation of residence with piers. At its maximum extent the building is exactly 100 feet wide in this view form the south.

From above, a view from the south revealing the two levels and their surrounding decks. The louver system displays a unique and compelling visual texture to the appearance of the building.

Residence Views

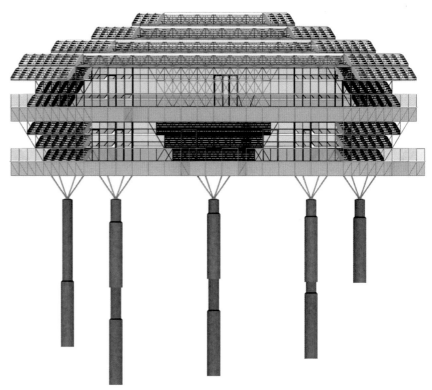

North elevation of the residence with piers. Stairways have been omitted from this view.

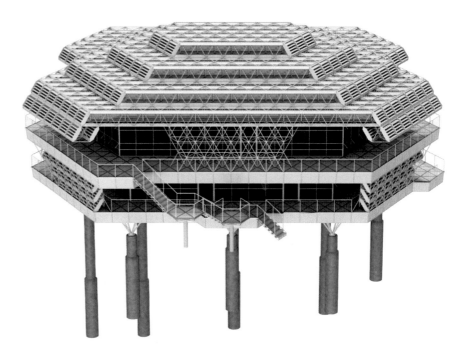

From above, as viewed from the north, showing the stairway, which enables access between the upper and lower levels of the residence, and access to grade not shown).

Residence Views

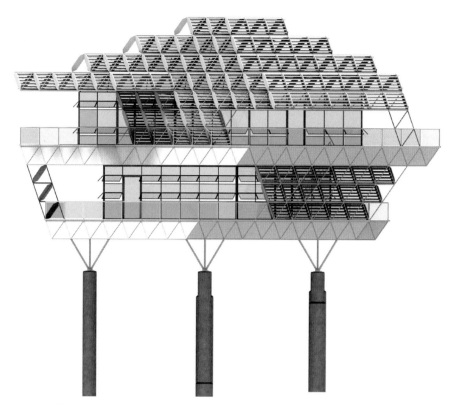

East elevation of residence with piers. Stairway is not shown.

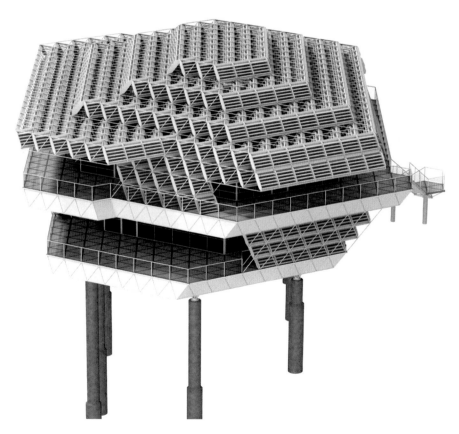

From above, a view from the east. Note that the louvers are oriented differently on the east (and west) facing side of the building to manage shade in the early morning hours when compared to the north side (left side of image).

Residence Plan

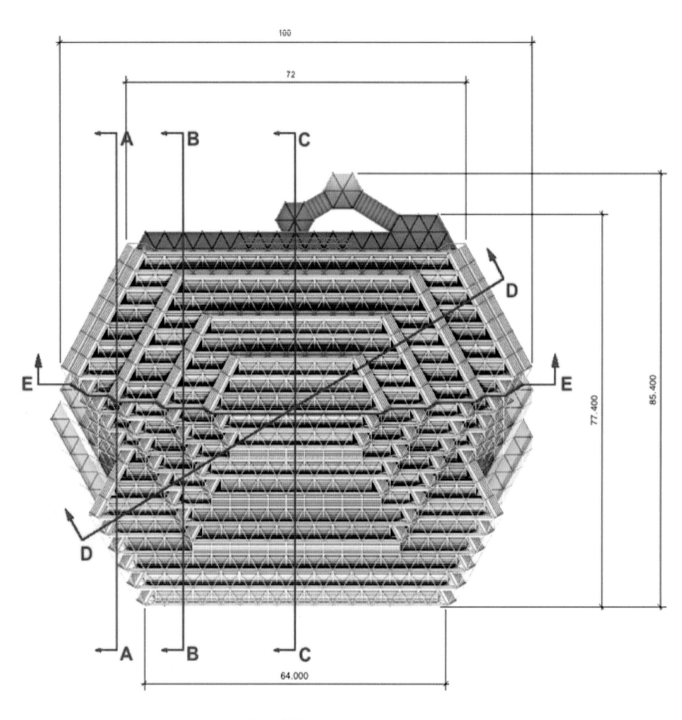

Roof Plan

Residence Plan with Sections

The site sections indicated above of the *Pearce Ecohouse* residence are shown in the following images. Dimensions are shown in feet.

Residence Sections

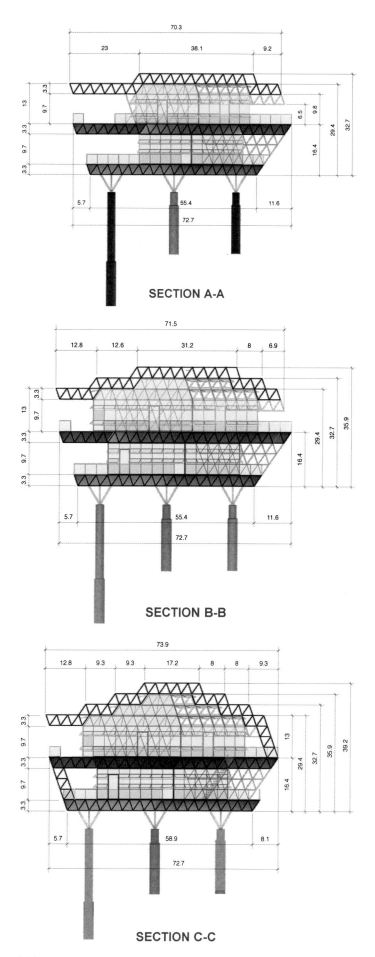

SECTION A-A

SECTION B-B

SECTION C-C

Residence Sections

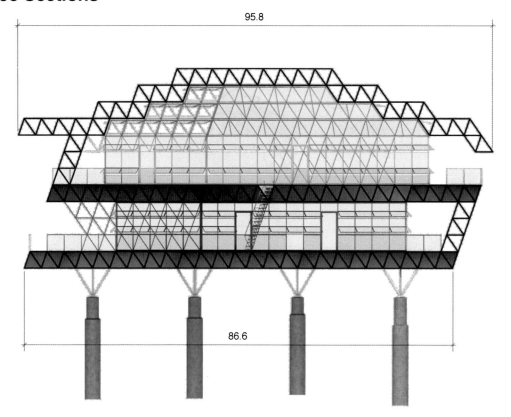

SECTION D-D

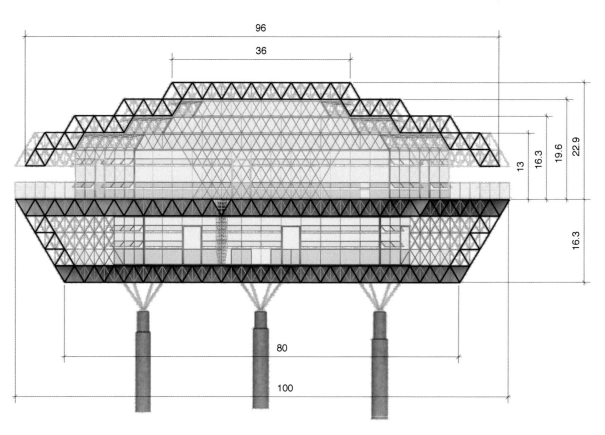

SECTION E-E

Garage Views

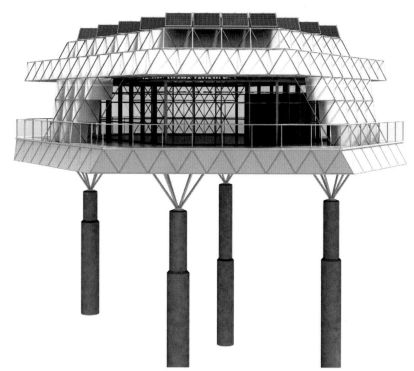

Garage from the south, with piers.

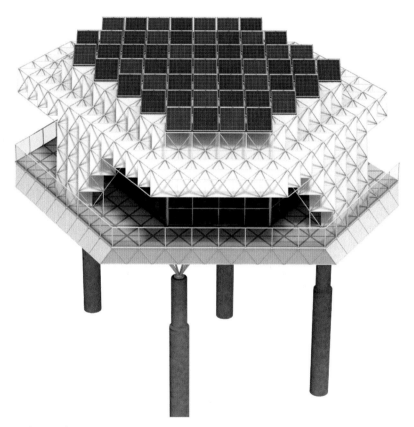

Garage from above, viewed from the south. Photovoltaic solar collectors are shown on the roof of the garage. The garage incorporates a different louver scheme from the residence. Because the garage is not considered a habitable building it does not require the same level of performance as does the residence. Therefore, the garage louvers are of simpler design, consisting of flat panels attached directly to the space truss.

Garage Views

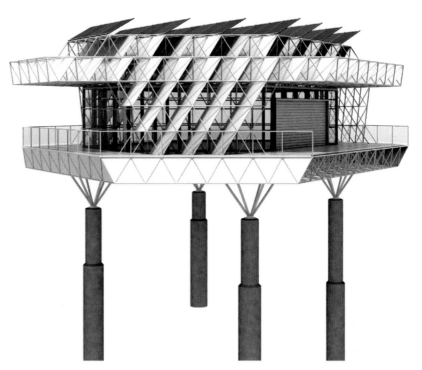

View from the southeast. The simplified louver scheme can be seen. Flat panels are incorporated that provide shade most of the year. The photovoltaic panels are outboard of the exoskeleton so the their display angle can be optimized.

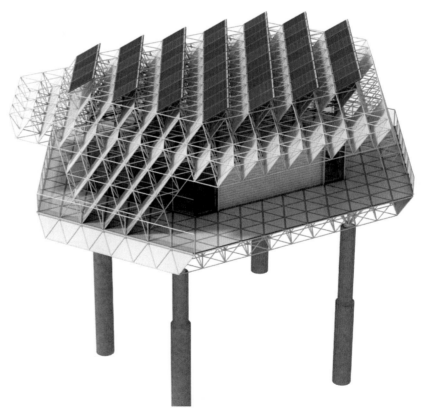

From above, a view from the east. Solar collectors are spaced and oriented so that they do not self-shade. Self-shading would reduce the daily and seasonal time of solar radiation exposure, which will compromise their production of electrical energy.

Garage Elevations

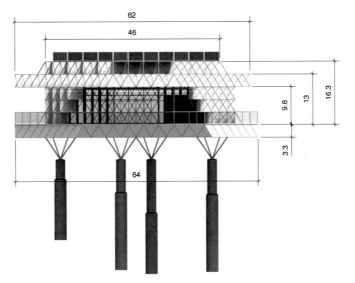

ELEVATION FROM THE SOUTH

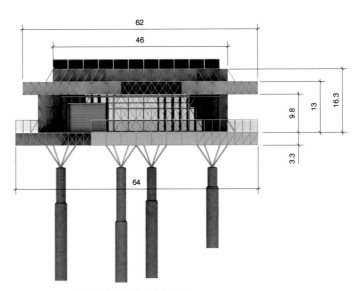

ELEVATION FROM THE NORTH

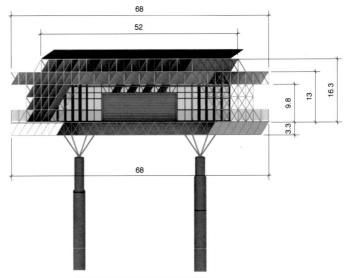

ELEVATION FROM THE NORTHEAST

Garage Elevations

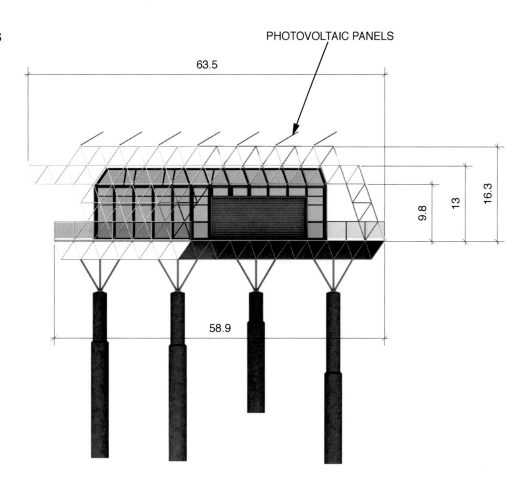

ELEVATION FROM THE EAST

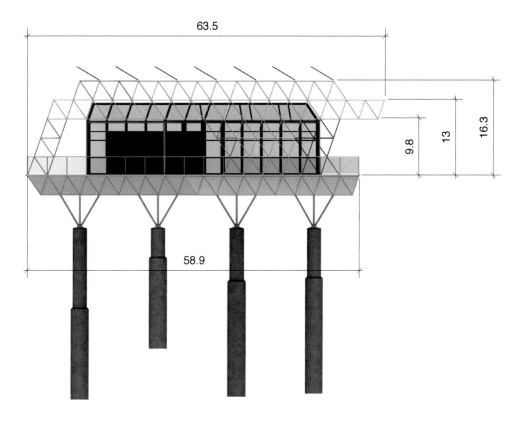

ELEVATION FROM THE WEST

117

Garage Plans

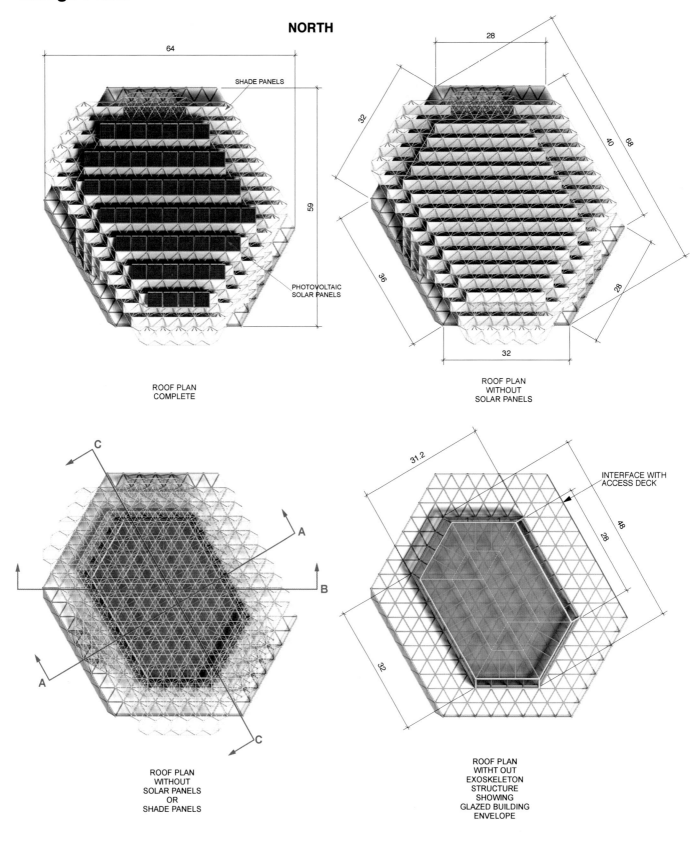

NORTH

64

SHADE PANELS

59

PHOTOVOLTAIC
SOLAR PANELS

ROOF PLAN
COMPLETE

28

32

40

68

36

28

32

ROOF PLAN
WITHOUT
SOLAR PANELS

C

A

B

A

C

ROOF PLAN
WITHOUT
SOLAR PANELS
OR
SHADE PANELS

31.2

INTERFACE WITH
ACCESS DECK

48

28

32

ROOF PLAN
WITHT OUT
EXOSKELETON
STRUCTURE
SHOWING
GLAZED BUILDING
ENVELOPE

Garage Sections

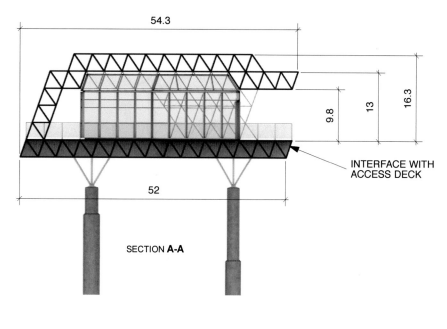

54.3

16.3

13

9.8

INTERFACE WITH
ACCESS DECK

52

SECTION **A-A**

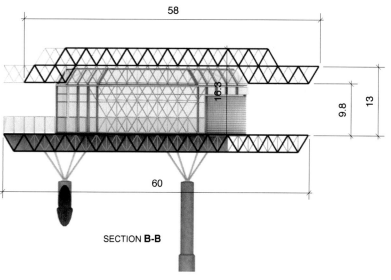

58

16.3

13

9.8

60

SECTION **B-B**

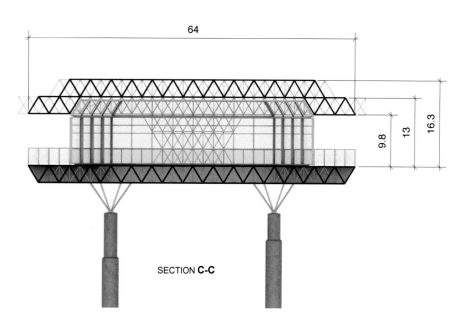

64

16.3

13

9.8

SECTION **C-C**

119

Access Deck Plan

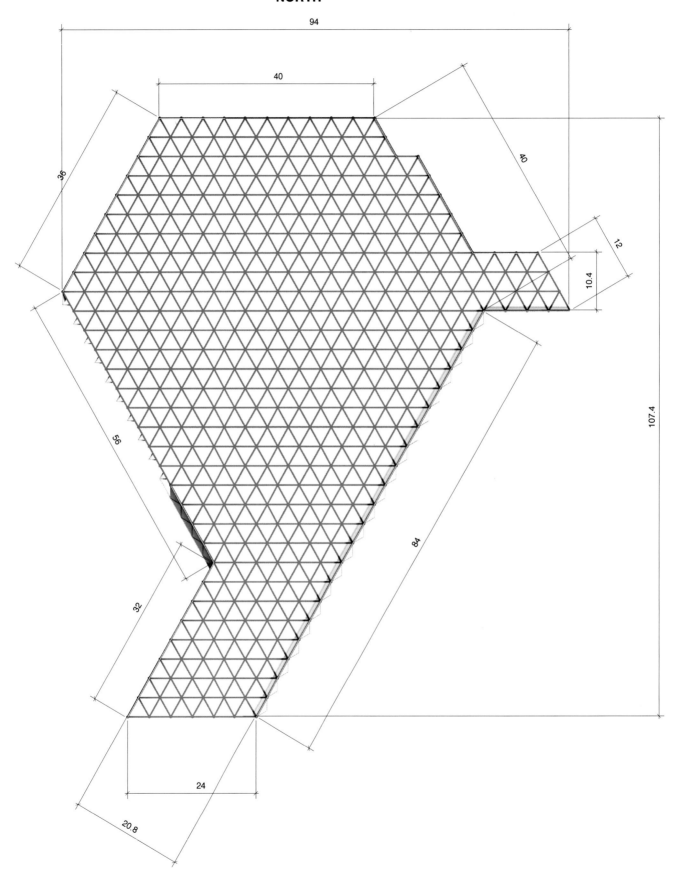

Access deck from the south.

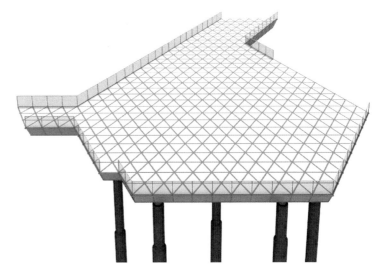

Access deck from the north.

Access deck from the east.

Revisiting the Design Elements

Having visualized the *Pearce Ecohouse* in the preceding pages, the reader is now familiar with the physical design of the project. In the following pages we reiterate in more detail the design concepts and features that comprise the essence of this net-zero energy residential design.

Building Spaces

As we have shown, the project consists of two building enclosures, a two level residence with 5439 square feet of interior space and a detached garage with 1217 square feet of interior space. In addition to these enclosures there is a large deck with 5228 square feet of plan area, which provides vehicular and pedestrian access to the garage and residence. The two enclosures are joined in a structural continuum by this access deck. This entire structural complex "floats" over an "ephemeral ravine", supported by poured-in-place concrete piles.

Building Enclosure

The building enclosure is comprised entirely of insulated glass, including all exterior walls, doors, and roof. In the case of the lower level, only the vertical walls are glass, since the floor deck of the upper level forms the ceiling/roof of the lower level. The glass enclosure of the upper level actually "hangs" from the exoskeleton space truss, forming a column-free interior space. The lower level is enclosed with vertical glass walls between the floor deck of the upper level and the floor deck of the lower level. A column-free space is also created for the lower level interior.

There are operable windows around the entire vertical perimeter walls of the upper and lower level enclosures, and operable windows in the overhead (roof) glazing. The vertical glazed walls enclosing the lower level are identical to the vertical glazing system used in the upper level. With the upper level, a large (3138 sq. ft.) open plan is formed with 360 degrees of view, including the ocean on the south, and the sky towards the north, with an interior flooded in natural reflected (indirect) light.

122

Upper Level

The two level residential building is of open plan design and is enclosed entirely with insulated glass, including walls and roof. The upper level, which is the main residential living area, is comprised of a floor deck supported by a planar three-dimensional truss system. Springing from this deck is a stepped truss system forming an "exoskeleton" structure. This exoskeleton, being outboard of the building enclosure, is supported on an extension of a space truss that forms the floor plane of the upper level. The exoskeleton springs directly from this deck from three zones, displaced on alternating sides of an elongated hexagonal plan form. The total deck area is 5874 square feet and the enclosed area of the upper level is 3138 square feet. It is possible to circumnavigate the entire building enclosure from the exterior zone of the deck.

Lower Level

The entire upper level floor deck, including the exoskeleton structure, is supported by three additional truss assemblies. These truss assemblies rise from a lower space truss, which forms the floor plane of the lower level. These truss assemblies are outboard of the lower level enclosure, enabling the circumnavigation of the deck from outside of the lower level enclosure. These support structures are found on alternating sides of the hexagonal plan form. The total deck area of the lower level is 4965 square feet, and the enclosed area within the deck plan is 2311 square feet.

Detached Garage

A detached garage is included, which, in every respect, is built with the same components as is the house structure. It is configured as an exoskeleton structure supporting a 100% glass enclosure, including walls and roof. The exoskeleton is populated by a louver scheme similar to that of the house, but is less sophisticated. The louver scheme for the garage provides shade but does not allow winter sun into the enclosure. Since the garage is not for human habitation, this simpler louver configuration is considered adequate.

Access Deck

Joining the residence structure with the garage structure is a large access deck, which spans over the "ephemeral ravine". The deck surface is coplanar with the upper level floor of the residence and the floor of the garage. This deck provides parking for access to the residence and the garage, as well as pedestrian access. It is also sufficiently large to provide the 60-foot diameter turnaround required by the LA County Fire Department. Like the garage, this structure is built from the same components, as is the house structure. The floor cladding over the supporting space truss is similar to the exterior decks surrounding the house and the garage.

Photovoltaic Array

A photovoltaic array is mounted on the garage roof with adequate capacity to provide all the electrical power required to supply the energy needs of this energy efficient all electric house. Because this system will be interactive with the electric grid, daily shortfalls of electricity will be made up from the grid. Such shortfalls will be counter balanced by excess production at other times. In so doing net-zero energy use will be achieved on an annualized basis.

The garage is the energy infrastructure for the entire *Pearce Ecohouse* project. It contains the components necessary to convert and distribute alternating current (AC) to the project. It also includes battery backup to cover power failure. The enclosed area of the garage is 1217 square feet. Like the residence the garage enclosure is supported by an exoskeleton, which rises directly off the space truss deck. The total plan area the this deck is 2768 square feet.

Interior Floor Cladding

The space truss deck interior floor structures are clad with a composite system consisting of triangular synthetic stone panels mounted onto cast aluminum panels which are attached directly to the space truss joints via special cast spiders. These panel assemblies are triangular in plan form. This floor system provides for thermal mass, location of hydronic tubing for radiant heat and cooling, vibration damping, high structural performance, long life, and cost effectiveness. Floor panel assemblies are in the form of equilateral triangles approximately 4 feet on a side, 3 inches thick, and correspond to the 4-foot triangular grid of the space truss deck. Once fastened to the joints of the space truss at the panel apices, they are separated by channels, which contain electrical and network cables for distribution throughout the house. The finish of the floor is integral to the synthetic stone panel.

Exterior Deck Cladding

Like the interior floor system, the exterior deck is clad in a modular panel system that matches the 4-foot triangular grid of its supporting space truss. These modular panels are identical aluminum castings, which provide for drainage control by directing run off from rain to a gutter system underneath the floor plane.

Interior Visualized

Upper Level Residential Space

The enclosed space has a plan area of 3138 square feet and a perimeter of 212 feet. The total deck area inclusive of interior and exterior has a plan area of 5576 square feet.

The upper level deck plan includes the interior living space and exterior perimeter. This deck is formed by a planar space-truss. A column-free open plan is provided for the interior space. Bathrooms are fully enclosed in combination with a utility core, which contains the infrastructure for utilities and plumbing. There are two bathrooms included in this spatial complex, which is topped with a glass ceiling to take advantage of the natural light entering the building through its 100%

Lower Level General-Purpose Space

Below the deck-floor structure of the upper level is an enclosed general purpose space of 2311 square feet, which is also hexagonal in plan form. The floor of the lower level space is comprised of the same space truss structural system and floor cladding system from which the upper level floor is built. This enclosed space is entirely column-free, which enables the flexible use of the space for a variety of functions in the future. It can be partitioned at will to create guest rooms, workspaces, and other spaces as may be desired. The enclosure of this space is accomplished with vertical glazed walls that are identical to the vertical glazing system used in the primary residential space of the upper level. As was previously mentioned, these glazed walls also have 84 operable windows.

Interior Spatial Differentiation

Functional spaces within the interior are differentiated with a movable modular storage wall partition system. The storage wall system can be configured in virtually any geometry to adapt to the functional requirements of the building residents. The system is constructed from an internal framework of aluminum extrusions, clad with aluminum panels. Any kind of storage from clothes-hanging to lateral files to shelves can be accommodated. The system includes an integral shelving system for books and other items and a cantilevered desk that mounts to the system. The system units measure 24 inches deep and 84 inches high, and comprises a lateral incremental dimension of 24 inches.

NORTH

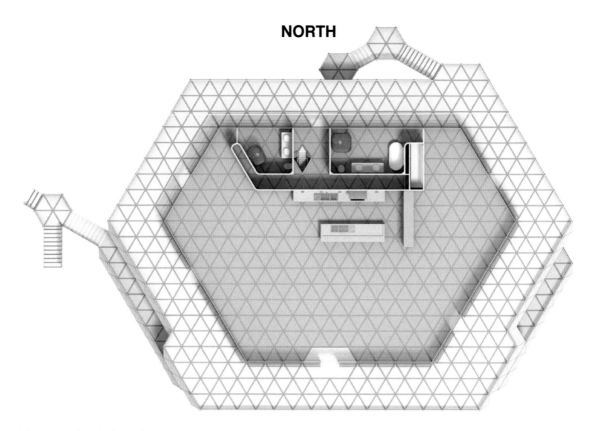

In this upper level plan view the interior space is shown unfurnished, without the functional spatial differentiation of the storage wall partition system. The kitchen, bathrooms, and utility space are "permanent" parts of the unfurnished space.

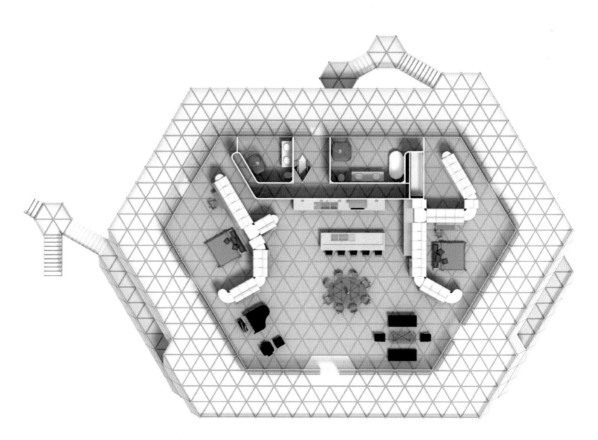

In this upper level plan view the interior space is shown fully furnished with the storage wall partition system differentiating functional spaces.

NORTH

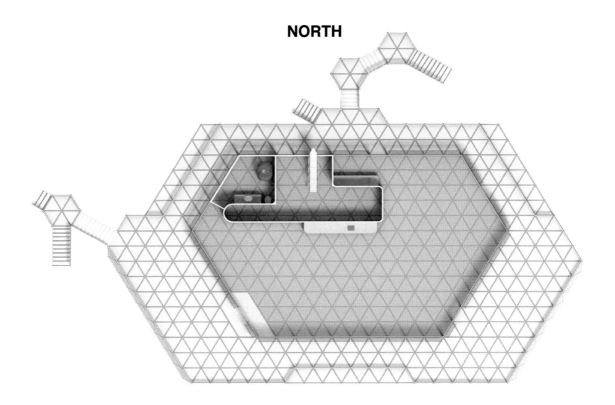

In this lower level plan view the interior space is shown unfurnished, without the functional spatial differentiation of the storage wall partition system. As in the uppoer level, the bathroom, and utility space are "permanent" parts of the unfurnished space.

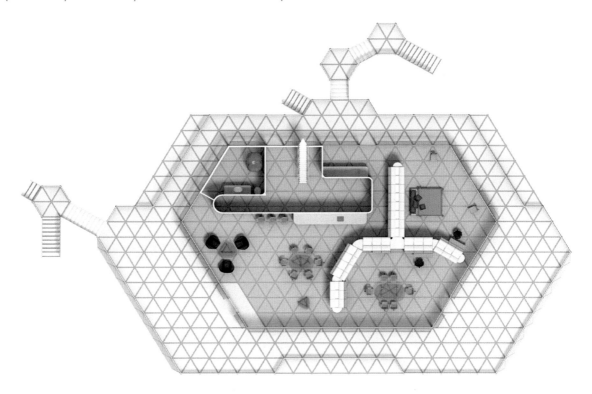

In this lower level plan view the interior space is shown fully furnished with the storage wall partition system differentiating functional spaces.

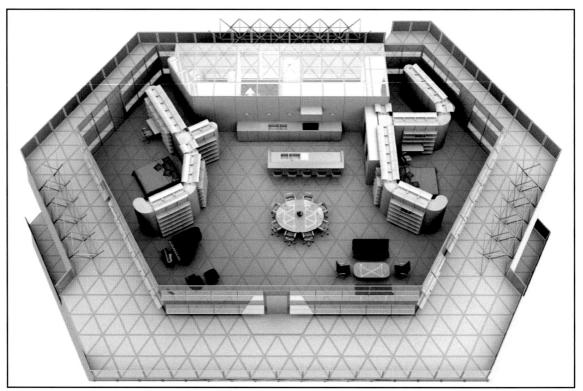

The upper level interior is shown in perspective from above with the roof system removed. This view is from the south. The glass ceiling enclosing two bathrooms and a utility core can be seen at the rear of the space. The kitchen is positioned in front of this bathroom/utility space enclosure. Centrally located in the space is the dining table as part of the open plan living area. The master bedroom is on the right and a guest room is on the left in this view.

The upper level view from the southwest. Note the integral book shelves mounted to the storage walls and located throughout the space. A cantilevered desk can be seen in the guest room. Along the top planes of the storage walls are attached parabolic lighting fixtures, which provide ambient light during night time.

Upper level space shown with an alternative interior plan. In the this case the guest room size has been reconfigured and two home office spaces have been added, which can be seen in the foreground. The color change in the floor denotes the exterior perimeter wall.

A closer in view showing a specially designed office desk system, which is compatible with the storage wall system. The parabolic lighting system on the top surface of the storage walls can be clearly seen in this image. Note the shelving system hanging from the storage walls.

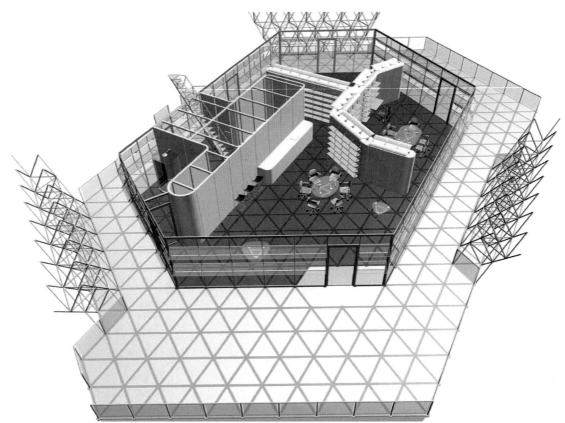

A view from the southwest showing the lower level interior space and exterior deck. Three structural buttresses which support the upper level can be seen on three edges of the deck. On the left can be seen the utility core including a utility stair that enables access between the upper level and lower level utility spaces. The enclosed space comprises 2311 sq. ft., and the exterior deck comprises 2654 sq. ft.

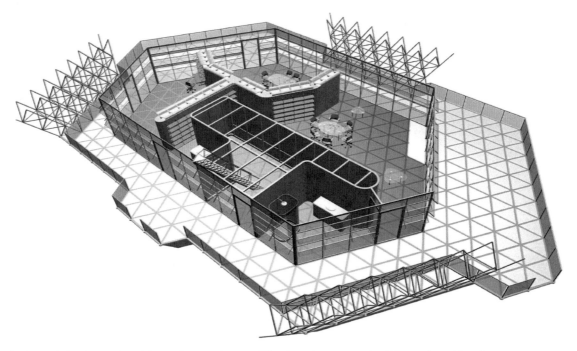

A view of the lower level from the northwest. The interior space is differentiated by the storage wall system as in the upper level. In this configuration a guest room is provided along with general-purpose spaces. One bathroom is provided in the lower level which is located in the northwest corner of the interior space.

Looking into the upper level space from the south. The open-plan general living space is in the foreground with the kitchen in the rear of the space. Although the clear span supporting exoskeleton can be seen overhead, remember that the glass enclosure is inboard of this structural system.

In this view we are looking toward the east through the open-plan living space. Some sunlight can be seen leaking through the overhead Climate Management Canopy, suggesting early October. In the left foreground can be seen the storage wall system wrapping around a corner, with the integral book shelf system hanging on its face.

In this view the living space is shown with Eames furniture in the foreground. The person on the right, which represents the author and designer of the *Pearce Ecohouse* is looking over some books on the shelves that are integral with the storage wall system.

Dining and kitchen areas are shown as part of the open-plan living space.

In this view of the interior, the kitchen is seen on the left, dining in the center, and sitting area in the right background. This architectural concept carries the idea of open-plan living space introduced with mid-century modernism to another level. This is possible due to completely column-free space provided by the structural system of the *Pearce Ecohouse*. The social architecture of this plan facilitates conversation through the entire living space of the house as activities may be unfolding in a non-hierarchical democratic interaction.

For example refreshment and food preparation, including clean up, can take place in the kitchen, without isolating the individuals involved in such activities. No one is isolated in the space enabling everyone to participate in whatever conversation or other activities may be taking place.

A view from the southeast with the supporting exoskeleton structures removed from the both the garage and the residence.

Moving in closer to the residence from the northeast. The simplicity of the glass enclosure is revealed.

From the southwest with structure and glass enclosure removed.

Close-in from the southeast, without enclosure. Color change on the floor differentiates interior from exterior spaces. The storage wall system is simple furniture added to the open-plan space.

These cutaway views reveal the anatomy of the *Pearce Ecohouse*. Although an unfamiliar way to build a residential structure has been developed, it is a fundamentally simple technology assembled from a kit of components that are entirely manufactured prior to delivery to the site.

Achieving Closure

Scope of Work

This document was completed in August 2015. As you read it you may wonder when the project will be completed? This is an important questions that is not easy to answer.

The scope of work to realize the *Pearce Ecohouse* is extensive. It is obvious from this document that the basic design is completed, pending minor revisions that are always possible. Furthermore, schematic design for most of the required components is also completed.

What is not completed is final detail design of all of the components required to build the house. In addition, geology and soils engineering, along with grading and drainage plans are not completed by appropriate consulting engineers. Also, permitting from county and state agencies, although in process, has not been completed. This latter issue requires the preparation of comprehensive "submittal packages", which include engineering calculations and reports, along with a complete and detailed drawing package. Actual site work cannot begin until permits are issued.

The project site, as has been previously mentioned, is in the Santa Monica Mountains of Los Angeles County, California. This site is found within the unincorporated county boundaries and, therefore, not governed by any city building codes. Rather the project is governed by Los Angeles County Department of Building and Safety. Included within this building code regime is LA County Department of Regional Planning, California Coastal Commission, and LA County Department of Building and Safety.

Preliminary approval has been granted from LA County Department of Regional Planning, but some significant revisions to the site plan requires a new submittal. This new submittal is complete except for the geology and soils engineering amendments. Once the updated planning package has been submitted we expect that it will take 24 to 36 months for final construction permits to be issued. We expect the remaining product development work to be completed within this window of time.

As has been indicated, the house is entirely constructed, or more accurately assembled, from a "kit-of-parts" that is custom designed and entirely manufactured off-site, ready to assemble. This is an extensive product development effort, which is being designed entirely using computer modeling. Physical prototypes are underway using advanced methods such as 3-D Printing, which is a version of rapid prototyping. Such prototype components, which are typically full scale, are used to verify the viability of all components.

Site work cannot begin until building permits are issued. Once site work is completed, which will take approximately eight weeks, including grading, drilling, and poured-in-place concrete piers, the building will be assembled. With a carefully planned "just-in-time" delivery schedule for all components, the building assembly is anticipated to take approximately eight weeks. This assembly process will be documented with time-lapse and still photography.

Once the building is completed, work will begin immediately to produce a book documenting the entire process from design through implementation. Although none of the physical details of the structural, floor, glazing, and louver systems are disclosed in this present preview document, these systems will be fully disclosed and explained in the subsequent book. In addition, it is hoped that we will be able to produce a documentary film on the project.

Once the Pearce Ecohouse is up and running, we will document its performance. Fundamentally, we will determine how much energy is consumed over an annual cycle, during which a temperate environment will be maintained. We will answer the question: does the *Pearce Ecohouse* perform as expected? Does it fulfil the promise of net-zero energy consumed on an annualized basis? Do the economics of its construction and life cycle costs make sense? We fully expect to answer these questions in the affirmative.

Rational Alternatives

This project is my attempt to realize an effort that began with my Graham Foundation Fellowship in 1965. My goal is to create rational alternatives to conventional building in the interest of high-performance design. My belief that this is possible has not been diminished in 50 years trying to achieve such objectives. The *Pearce Ecohouse* will be the first project that truly embodies my vision of what is possible.

Modest House

Although this project is just a "simple" and modest house, I trust that fundamental principles will be demonstrated that can be applied to virtually any building project of any scale. The *Pearce Ecohouse* will demonstrate efficient high-performance structural systems and minimum energy climate management strategies, while providing a sense of well-being through access to daylight, natural ventilation, and a flexible open architecture.

Sense of Well Being

I have suggested that an important goal of the *Pearce Ecohouse* is to provide a sense of well being for the people living in this environment. I have argued that the minimum conditions for achieving such a goal is the maintenance of a temperate of environment. However, equally important is access to natural light, natural ventilation, and what could be called a communion with nature. The question becomes what will it be like to live in the Pearce Ecohouse? Of course this will partly be question of personal preference, but there may be some universal values that manifest themselves.

There is very good fortune in this because the project site is exceptional. Beyond the interesting (and challagning) topography, there are great views of the Santa Monica Bay, and, as we have seen, the property is covered with beautiful native plants. All this speaks to the communion with nature. We have seen the landscaping with the terrain and plants earlier in this document, and dynamically spectacular views occur, especially in the winter months. We include here some examples of sunrises and sunsets that have been viewed from this 2200 foot elevation.

141

Sunrise looking toward Santa Monica, with the Santa Monica Bay on the right from January 2011.

Sunset looking west to the Pacific Ocean from September 2014.

Of course the *Pearce Ecohouse* is designed to take advantage of this potential for experiencing nature. Not only is the siting of the residence ideal, but the extensive use of glass as a fundamental enclosure material is a key attribute. This almost total transparency of the enclosure means the communion with nature is the default experience. This is true not only for the obvious lateral view opportunities, but for overhead views. Although the louvers and its supporting exoskeleton occlude the view overhead, there is visible sky that can be seen through the overhead structures. By looking through the louvers the north sky is readily visible. This, in combination with the vertical glass, enables the nuances of nature's thrilling weather dynamics to be appreciated and enjoyed. Indeed, for me, this is nothing less than a spiritual experience. A sense of well being is readily at hand.

For those that may be worried about privacy, all the vertical glass of the enclosure will have integrated cellular blinds. In addition to providing a method for creating a privacy, the cellular blinds double the U-value of the glass enclosure panels. These blinds can be adjusted to modulate incoming sunlight as well.

Beyond the intrinsic advantages of the project site relative to these opportunities for communion with nature, there are other design features that have the potential to contribute to a sense of well being. These include an abundance indirect natural light and natural ventilation. These are attributes destined to create a friendly environment. The open column-free plan of the *Pearce Ecohouse* enhances the benefits of both natural light and ventilation.

Moral Obligation

In the final analysis, it is the moral obligation of all designers to strive for a responsible use of energy - to break our dependence on fossil fuels - and to create habitats and products, which are based on durable intrinsic values consistent with effective stewardship of the natural environment. The *Pearce Ecohouse* is my attempt to be responsive to such goals.

Peter Jon Pearce
Malibu, California
August 2015

Index

A

Abusive development, 9, 61
Acoustic privacy, 64
Agent of performance, v, 5, 8, 10, 31
Air conditioning, 26-27, 40, 43, 94
Airtight, 12, 28, 37, 80
Airflow, 43
Aluminum, 36, 43, 48, 74, 79, 80, 84, 125
Architectural attributes, 29
Axis, 41

B

Borings, 38, 74, 79
Building system, 4, 11, 31, 58, 61

C

California, 40, 41, 47, 54
Cast-in-place, 74,
Catalina Island, 54
Ceanothus, 57
Channel Islands, 54
Chaparral, 47
Circumnavigate, 66, 123
Clear span, 12, 35, 133
Climate management canopy, 7
Co-planar, 64
Column capitals, 37-38, 67, 73,
Components, 97, 104, 123-24, 38-39
Composite, 138-139
Computer aided design, 39
Concentrated loads, 38, 73, 104
Concrete, 35, 38, 48, 74-75, 79, 122, 140
Conductor, 36
Connection system, 61,
Contours, 58, 61,
Convection currents, 43,
Conventional construction, 34
Cross-ventilation, 43
Clear span, 35, 133, 12

D

Design adaptation, 58
Design simplicity, 29
Design strategy, 8, 11, 23, 32, 57
Differentiation,124, 79, 127-129,
Drought-tolerant, 30, 46-48, 96-97

E

Ecosystem, 12, 30, 47-49, 57, 80
Ephemeral ravine, 56, 35, 37, 40, 76, 77, 80,
    82, 85, 88, 92, 111, 124, 133

F

Factory-made, 34
Fire ecology, 48
First principles, 10-11, 23, 28, 31
Form as an agent of performance, v, 5, 8

G

Geological, 30, 54
Geometry, 6,12, 30, 47, 57, 80 32, 41, 58,
    79, 82, 127
Geothermal, 28, 36, 42-43, 78-79
Global warming, 5, 6
Green building, 34
Green design, 7, 33

H

Habitat, 12, 24, 28, 48-49, 57-58, 143
Heat exchanger, 42, 78-79
Heat gain, 26, 40-41, 44, 86, 92-93,
Heat pump, 36, 41-42, 78-79
Heat transfer, 29
Heating, 28-29, 36, 40-42, 78, 94
High-energy, 6
High performance, 7-8, 10-12, 23, 35, 141,
High-strength-to-weight, 4, 28, 35,
Holly Leaf Cherry, 57
Honeycomb, 10
Human culture, 8
Hydronic tubing, 36, 41

I

Insulated glass, 37. 44, 66, 80, 81, 122, 123,
Integrated product, 28, 66
Intervention, 28, 30, 48-49, 57-58, 66,96
Inverters, 29, 78
Irrational, 9

J

Just-in-time, 74, 140

K

Kit-of-parts, 4, 34 ,39, 74, 140

L

Lateral stability, 60
Laurel Sumac, 57
Louver scheme, 68, 86, 92, 114-116 123
Low density, 47

M

Manzanita, 57
Mediterranean climate, 47, 49
Mesa Verde, 24-25
Microclimate, 43, 47
Minimal surface, 44
Minimum site intervention, 28, 30, 38, 48, 57
Modular, 29, 33, 53, 81, 79, 25, 12
Moral imperative, 6
Morphological principles, 54
Morphology, 11, 23

N

Native habitat, 28, 49, 57-58
Natural cooling, 27
Natural light, 4, 24, 44, 85, 126, 141, 143
Natural structure, 10
Net-zero, 28-29, 43, 78, 122 140, 142,
Non-depletable, 5

O

Off-the-shelf, 39
Open plan, 4, 28-29, 53, 80, 122-123, 137, 126, 130, 133-135
Operable windows, 37, 43, 66, 80, 122, 126
Orientation, 41
Outboard sprinklers, 37, 80
Overheating, 40, 94

P

Paradigm shift, v, 7-8, 26
Parameter, 24, 32
Passive, 25, 28-29, 41, 53, 92,
Pearce Structures, 12,13
Perimeter, 37, 43, 80-81, 122, 126, 131
Phenomenon: 80/20, 34
Photovoltaic, 28-29, 77-78, 96, 104, 114, 117, 118, 124
Piers, 7, 35, 58, 67, 96, 104, 107, 114, 140
Pre-glazed, 80
Prefabricated, 28, 34, 79
Product design, 3, 30, 39, 74, 83
Preservation, 28, 30, 57
Purpose, 23-24, 26, 28, 126, 132

R

Radiant heating, 28, 36, 41-42, 78, 94
Rapid prototyping, 39, 140
Redshank, 57
Regional codes, 54
Residents, 29-30, 66, 68, 127

S

Santa Monica Mountains 4, 46-47, 54, 139
Seepage pits, 79
Seismic, 38
Semi-wilderness, 47
Septic, 78-79,
Service cores, 64, 79
Shelters, 23-24
Silicone, 12, 37, 39, 80
Site, 79-80, 96-98, 100, 104, 110, 138, 143
Solar thermal, 29, 96
Solar radiation, 25-26, 40-41, 43, 53, 85-86, 88-93, 115
Space-truss, 13, 35, 37-38, 68, 82, 85, 126
Spatial, 24, 29, 33, 53, 61, 79, 126-129
Spatial vocabulary, 61
Stack effect, 43
Strength of geometry, 32
Structural analysis, 39, 51
Structure in Nature is a Strategy for Design, 11
Strut components, 35, 61, 89
Super-structure, 35
Surface area, 13, 36 ,44
Surface to volume, 44
Sustainable, 5, 7
Synthetic, 36, 41, 74, 79, 125

T

Temperate, 24, 26-27, 29 140-141
Temperature, 26-27,36, 38, 40, 78, 92, 94
Terra forming, 61
Terrain, 38-38, 68, 96, 141
Thermal mass, 36, 41, 125
Three dimensional, 35, 85, 123
Topography, 30, 38, 48-49, 58, 97- 98, 141
Topologically complex, 54
Toyon, 57
Truss assemblies, 67, 123
Tubular steel struts, 12, 61
Turnaround, 64, 124

U

U-value, 44
Underground, 42, 78-79
Upper level, 60, 64, 66, 72, 76-77, 80, 90
User friendly, 29
Utility space, 29, 89, 128-130, 132
Utility stairway, 64

V

Vocabulary, 31, 61

W

Well-being, 24, 27, 29, 49, 141

Z

Zero grading, 28, 30

Made in the USA
Middletown, DE
18 October 2021

50573350R00093